PLAY WORK

Michael Townsend Smith

PLAY WORK

a life in theatre

FAST BOOKS

Fast Books are edited and published by Michael Smith
P. O. Box 1268, Silverton, OR 97381

ISBN 978-0-9982793-2-9

Copyright © 2017 by Michael Townsend Smith

To the Reader

Welcome!

I am happy that you are reading these words and hope you find this brief account of my life and work in theatre edifying and entertaining.

My play work won awards and often provoked good reviews, but despite exquisite productions, none of my plays had any popular success: it was all succés d'estime. Hence my creative output, except as a critic, has all but vanished from theatrical history as well as the living stage. This text reaffirms its expressive intentions.

Most of my scripts, including a few that have not yet been produced, are available for reading on my website, michaeltownsendsmith.com, as well as in two volumes self-published by Fast Books. *Michael Smith Plays I* covers the years 1964-1971, when I was living in New York and active in the off-off-Broadway theatre. *Michael Smith Plays II* contains later work staged in Santa Barbara and rural Oregon.

I also discuss my directing, producing, and lighting work, all of it part of the same artistic project.

This is probably the sum of my play work. Sans reputation and career, the only way I can get a show on is by producing, directing, designing, and lighting it myself, which was too much even when I was decades younger.

Silverton, Oregon
June 2017

in loving memory of
Alfred Brooks & Maxine Munt

The Plays

Act I 9

Refugees

I Like It

Directing: *A Sleep of Prisoners, The Hungerers, Three Sisters Who Are Not Sisters, Icarus's Mother*

The Next Thing

More! More! I Want More!

Lighting: *A Funny Walk Home*

Vorspiel nach Marienstein

Directing: *Chas. Dickens's Christmas Carol, Donovan's Johnson, With Creatures Make My Way, Vorspiel nach Marienstein, The Life of Juanita Castro, Dr. Kheal, Hurricane of the Eye*

Captain Jack's Revenge

Act II 37

A Dog's Love

Tony

Peas

Directing: *Eat Cake, XXXXX*

Country Music

Directing: *Bigfoot, Tango Palace*

Double Solitaire

Prussian Suite

A Wedding Party
Cowgirl Ecstasy

Act III   61

Directing: *Krapp's Last Tape* and *The Zoo Story, West Side Story, Life Is Dream*
Heavy Pockets
Half Life
Translation: *Agatha*
Directing: *A Shot in the Dark, Curse of the Starving Class*
One Hundred Thousand Songs
Trouble
Lighting: *I and I, The Tablets, Rules of Civility, Ancient Boys*
Life Before Death
Lighting: *The Zero Method*

Act IV   87

The Dinner Show
Fast Forward
Producing: *Trouble, Buried Child, Criminal Genius* and *Featuring Loretta, Escape from Happiness*
Dogs Bark All Night
Directing: *The Danube, Krapp's Last Tape*
Lighting: *Kiss of the Spider Woman, Happiness*
Turnip Family Secrets

Act V 107

Translation: *Victor, or Power to the Children*

Directing: *Beyond Therapy, A Midsummer Night's Dream (Abbreviated), The Flight of the Butter Boy*

Producing: *Trouble*

Lighting: *Blue Heart, Far Away, The Goat, or Who Is Sylvia?, The God of Hell*

Bad Dog and Other Plays

Summer Lightning

Hamlet in Love

Photo Credits 127

A Little Backstory

My beautiful mother sang and danced in the Junior League Follies in Kansas City, Missouri, in the early 1930s. All the women in her family played the piano. Her younger brother, my Uncle Alfred, went to Juilliard, studied composition with Nadia Boulanger in France after the war, became a composer, dancer, and choreographer in New York, and later a theatrical producer in Denver. My sister Virginia is an actress and taught theatre in a boarding school for thirty years, directing hundreds of plays. We were a conventional, respectable, thoroughly bourgeois family, but a taste for theatre ran in my blood.

Theatre was at the center of the culture while I was growing up in the heart of America. My mother accompanied my handsome father to New York on his regular business trips, and they kept up with the new shows, bringing me matchcovers from swanky Manhattan restaurants and nightclubs, programming me from an early age to view New York as a paradigm of glamor and sophistication. Mother brought home sheet music, which was sold in Broadway lobbies in those days, so she could play and sing the latest songs.

The national tours of hit musicals regularly stopped at the plush, deco Municipal Auditorium in downtown Kansas City. I was thirteen when my parents took me to see *Brigadoon*, with its lilting Lerner and Loewe songs, poignant love story, and dramatic ballet choreographed by Agnes de Mille. In the summers we went to the Starlight Theatre in Swope Park and saw old-fashioned operettas—*Rose-Marie, Desert Song, The Student Prince.* The stage was so wide that the curtain was a solid structure on wheels that rolled apart into the wings, which made a great impression on me. I saw a puppet production of *Hansel and Gretel* in the jewel-box theatre at the Nelson-Atkins Museum and got a peek backstage afterwards that marked me for life.

From sixth grade on I attended a private school, Pem-Day. I was on the stage crew for Gilbert and Sullivan's *Patience* and played the First Citizen in *Julius Caesar*. Good with electricity and machines, I often served as projectionist in the school auditorium, threading up and running the temperamental 16mm. projector, foreshadowing endless hours of tech work in later years.

My parents sent me east to prep school for the last two years before college. At Hotchkiss, an all-boys boarding school, I played Lord Stanley in a gray wig in *Richard III*; Queen Quinevere in a gown and veil in *A Connecticut Yankee* (I sang "Spring Is Here," relishing the innuendo); and raffish Sidney Carlton, the Noel Coward figure, in T*he Man Who Came to Dinner*, sitting down at the piano and tossing off a song.

Acting made me too nervous and self-conscious and gave me nightmares. At Yale I joined the Dramat as a light man, as recounted below. For the rest of my life I would find ways to work on plays without actually appearing on the stage myself.

Act I

Refugees

I always wanted to be a writer. I was happy to write anything to get into print, and it eventually gave me a livelihood, mostly as a journalist. I assumed my "own" writing would be novels, but it turned out I didn't have the patience for fiction. Plays are much easier—shorter, for one thing, and you don't have to write out all the machinery of narrative and description and scene-setting. You don't even have to describe the characters—actors do that for you: there they are, in the flesh, wearing the clothes. Dialogue is not a problem. Someone says something, which naturally provokes a response. The action is mostly entrances and exits. Someone comes in, and you have a scene.

My first play, *Refugees*, is a two-character one-act I wrote when I was twenty-five. I'm not sure anyone has ever read it. I was insecure and may have thought it was too naked an exercise in coming of age, too direct, too clumsy and obvious. I never tried to get it staged.

Refugees is transparently the story of Oedipus killing his father at the crossroads. An older man and a younger man, fleeing from the city and a revolution gone wrong, meet in a barren, fought-over wasteland. Their confrontation leads to the older man forcing the younger man to kill him—in order to go on.

I was living alone, a junior theatre critic at *The Village Voice*, just starting to make a life. The play has a modernist, bare-stage, minimalist style, obviously in thrall to *Waiting for Godot*—a quasi-realist, neo-primitive, post-everything fable. Like *Oedipus*

Rex, the action has political context and ambitions beyond the personal. The sense of bold idealism failing is painful. The image is of youth stepping into manhood by denying its origin, which at the time seemed to be obligatory.

I Like It

This saucy little romp was my first published play, included in an issue of *Kulchur* magazine guest-edited by a friend of mine. In a smart-alecky, "witty" style, it depicts the other side of the Oedipus situation: a character very much like the author is in bed with his mother, who is a little bit like mine, carrying on a frivolous conversation that turns curiously sharp at times. I wrote it as a joke, dedicating it to my psychoanalyst as an ironic farewell offering: not denying but embracing my Oedipal desires, showing them cheerfully realized. (The dedication "To J. C." refers not to either of my good friends Joe Chaikin or Joe Cino, much less Jesus Christ, but to Dr. John Cederquist.)

Proud to be in print, I sent a copy of the magazine to my mother, who told me later that she was so upset by my play that she burst into tears and threw it into the fire. It now seems obvious that what bothered her about *I Like It*, apart from the play's general rudeness, was that it mocked her diligent, wholly admirable charitable activities and understandably hurt her feelings.

I showed my play to Joe Cino, the ebullient, encouraging proprietor of the Caffè Cino on Cornelia Street, an Italian coffee house that provided a stage for countless new plays in the early 1960s, and he gave me a date to put it on. The Cino proved to be my portal to the high romantic gay bohemianism of Greenwich Village, a milieu I threw myself into wholeheartedly for the next decade. Denis Deegan, my roommate from Yale and longtime friend, helped me carry my own bed the four blocks from my apartment on West Third Street to the Cino and acted the part of the young man.

I Like It played nine performances in June 1963, the first play of mine to be produced. It was directed by Roberta Sklar, a member of the Open Theatre, who doesn't remember doing it. I don't remember much about it either, although I must have watched it multiple times with the coffee house audiences. Immediately after the play closed, before I had time to process the experience, I went to Europe for the first time—Rome! Spoleto! Paris! I retain an image of the blooming young man and attractive older woman, brightly lit, sitting up in bed side by side, incestuous and proud of it. That was the picture I wanted to show, think what you will, and there it was.

I am embarrassed by this callow, shallow, self-conscious, pretentious little play, its smug, brittle attitude a bad imitation of Noel Coward. The twee tone reflects the snooty attitudes I had temporarily fallen in with by way of prep school, the Ivy League, and my upper-class girlfriend Serena Stewart, before I escaped that aspect of myself into the classless bohemia of Greenwich Village. I nonetheless have let it stand as an artifact of its moment in my life. *I Like It* was republished in *Return to the Caffè Cino*, 2007, but omitted from my collected plays, and has occasionally been revived. I haven't reread it in years; possibly it is better than I think.

Directing
A Sleep of Prisoners, The Hungerers, Three Sisters Who Are Not Sisters, Icarus's Mother

As a boy I was always a good student, but in my late teens I lost my grip on schoolwork. Taking a "medical" leave of absence from Yale at Thanksgiving of my junior year, I found refuge, on my father's urging, at the Austen Riggs Center, a high-class psychiatric sanatorium in Stockbridge, Massachusetts, where I remained for nine months. The Freudian therapy never got to the point, somehow—my problem was not neurosis so much as youth and inexperience (i.e., virginity). However, Riggs's activities director, Dick Spahn, mentored me in directing a play with a cast of fellow patients, and that would set my life on its course.

Christopher Fry's *A Sleep of Prisoners* is a beautiful, poetic anti-war play. I loved staging it, imagining the action in space, telling the actors where to stand and what to do, encouraging them to memorize their parts, helping them to find the sense of their characters and make the imaginary real. The action is set in a church in wartime. We performed in a big upstairs room at Riggs's activities building. I remember feeling bold and modern in bringing the action out around the audience, using the whole room as a stage. We took the production to the Berkshire One-Act Play Festival at the public library in Pittsfield and won first prize.

Directing came to me naturally. I had no end of spontaneous ideas and energy to pursue them. This was something I could be good at and enjoy. I directed a second play at Riggs—*The Hungerers*, a one-act by William Saroyan—and decided to pursue directing as a career. For that, Dick Spahn told me, I would have to go to New York and should study acting, which would help me understand actors. Thus in August 1956 I moved to New York and enrolled at Stella Adler's acting academy, signing up for her famous class in characterization and scene study as well as regular classes in speech, singing, and ballet. A veteran of the Yiddish theatre and early member of the Group Theatre, Stella had studied with Stanislavski and transmitted his late ideas, privileging imagination over memory. Warren Beatty was a fellow student; we played the piano for each other's song practice. Stella herself was a lesson in theatricality. Dreading her attention, completely lacking any confidence in myself as a performer, I cowered on the fringes of the large roomful of eager students. Thinking I should at least try, I went so far as to audition for a television commercial, but I felt foolish and inept, surer than ever that I did not want to be an actor.

There was no obvious way to get started as a director. It never occurred to me to go back to college. Instead I gradually constructed a life and personality in the city, made friends with a few theatre people, and before long found myself reading scripts for a Broadway producer, which I was certainly not qualified to do. In the summer of 1957 Serena's friend Betty Rollin introduced me to Dan Wolf and Ed Fancher, the editor and publisher of *The Village Voice*, a hip new weekly newspaper in Greenwich Village, and I began writing, proofreading, editing, and reviewing plays for *The Voice*, which would be my main job for the next 17 years.

In the 1950s there was little theatre in New York outside of

Broadway and a few off-Broadway theatres mostly devoted to revivals of classics. Aspiring actors and directors were starved for opportunities to practice their craft, and playwrights had no place to try out their ideas. Thus a rush of new talent emerged when, beginning with the Caffè Cino, the do-it-yourself "downtown" theatre movement later known as Off-Off-Broadway came into existence in the early 1960s, offering free makeshift stages and open-minded audiences if no possibility of financial reward. Writing for *The Voice*, I paid close attention to this new work and came to know many of the key players.

The first opportunity I had to direct a play in New York was as part of a benefit for the Caffè Cino, which had suffered a catastrophic fire in March 1965. Ron Link, who had directed plays at the Caffè Cino, was the stage manager of *The Fantasticks* and arranged for us to use their theatre on a "dark" Monday night. I directed *Three Sisters Who Are Not Sisters* by Gertrude Stein, an antic deconstruction of family in the form of a murder melodrama too silly to take seriously. I put together a cast of five and scrupulously followed  the text in staging the action. Stein had written "Curtain" at the ends of scenes, but there was no curtain at the Sullivan Street Playhouse. So my friend Gwen Fabricant made a good-sized painting of a curtain, and I had my friends Johnny Dodd and Charles Stanley carry it across the stage at appropriate moments. Johnny and Charles had recently bleached their long dark hair blond, and made quite an effect. I enjoyed directing as much as I had before, difficult though it could be at times, with uncomfortable elements of ego-trip. Following the one-night benefit, the production transferred for two weekends to Judson Poets' Theatre.

Sam Shepard, then twenty-two, had burst upon the downtown theatre scene with a flurry of short plays, which I had reviewed at Theatre Genesis, La Mama, and Judson Church. To my mind he was the most exciting new playwright of my generation. Sam gave me a new play of his to direct at the Caffè Cino in November 1965.

Icarus's Mother is a simple one-act about five friends enjoying a picnic in a seaside park. Tripping, perhaps, probably on LSD—

we all were in those days—they are thrown into a paranoid panic by the noisy apparition of a jet plane overhead, which I imagined to be an embodiment of our ever-present fears of a nuclear bomb. Caught up in their fantasies, they play at being Native Americans, attempting to send smoke signals from their barbecue. As their delirium reaches its apex, the plane crashes into the ocean.

I never knew what the title meant, but I believed in Sam as a writer and did the play as he had written it. I had ideas about space, light, dynamics, and theatrical effects, covered the little platform stage with artificial grass, and fussed endlessly with the sound effects and trying to get smoke to come out of the barbecue on cue. I had almost no skill or experience directing actors, though. I learned a key lesson from working with these five, members of Joe Chaikin's Open Theatre and serious about their craft: that actors need to play the action (in this case the picnic, to begin with), not the presumptive meanings behind it, which will emerge in the audience's mind if the art is honest.

The Next Thing

In *Refugees* I had killed my father; in *I Like It* I slept with my mother; and in *The Next Thing*, my first long play, I murdered her. Introducing *The Next Thing* in an anthology I subsequently edited, immodestly titled *The Best of Off-Off-Broadway*, I hoped this play would be "my last study in family hang-ups." This was foolish, of course: family is one of the great subjects of drama, which I would come back to many times, never so claustrophobically as in these first plays.

There are three main characters in *The Next Thing*. Arthur, pushing middle age, lives with his wheelchair-bound mother in an old-fashioned, stuffy New York apartment. This evening, with uncharacteristic boldness, Arthur has invited a young woman home for dinner. Sue appears on crutches, her legs paralyzed. In the course of the evening, Arthur will shoot his mother, covering her afterwards with a sheet, and Sue will throw away her crutches and walk. This bizarre tale of peculiarly ironic liberation is briefly interrupted by a raving African-American man, Harold, the husband of their cook, who has disappeared, a reminder that this airless interior is not all there is to the world.

My intention in writing *The Next Thing* was to gradually build up a higher and higher level of emotional intensity, sustaining an almost unbearable ecstasy like a Strauss opera—specifically *Elektra*, which Joe Chaikin had played for me in Inge Borkh's electrifying performance. I still remember her cry of recognition: "Oreste!" My play was unified in time and space, constructed in three nearly continuous scenes, before, during, and after dinner. The actual shooting was not shown. The action was meant to unfold with stately inevitability. Whether this would have worked we will never know. Midway through rehearsals for the first production—sponsored by the Open Theatre at La Mama in March 1966—Jacques Levy, the director, cut up the script and and scotch-taped it back together into eleven scenes that jumped backward and forward in  time, a very different effect. Jacques would have quit if I didn't accede to this transformation, and I liked the result, which was challengingly experimental and radically unstable. Ostensibly a realistic domestic drama, the play is in reality a Greek tragedy and needed to be stylized.

Arthur is obviously a stand-in for the author, but the situation in the play in no way resembled my own actual life. I made it up out of stereotypes and assumptions. There is something deeply perverse about it and weirdly mocking—two crippled women competing for one man's soul and body. The play is an homage to Strindberg and Sartre, showing individuals trapped in their selfhood, struggling desperately to escape.

Jacques was a brilliant director, and his production of *The Next Thing* had considerable power, if I do say so myself. I was disappointed that Joe Chaikin could not be persuaded to play Arthur. Ed Setrakian was good but Joe's charm and brightness would have made the character more likable. Barbara Vann and Kay Carney gave defining performances as Mother and Sue. Robert Cosmos Savage composed and performed demented harpsichord music in the blackouts between scenes.

Looking in on a performance of *The Next Thing* one night tripping on acid, I recognized the three people glowing, moving, and talking on the stage at the end of the room as not only real but superreal, living, breathing, talking inhabitants of a deeply peculiar world I had made from nothing. It struck me as wildly funny.

More! More! I Want More!

Longer plays evolve over time. Short-form works can occur spontaneously. Hanging out with lighting designer John P. Dodd and author-artist Remy Charlip one day in October 1965, I mentioned playwright Robert Patrick's call for five-minute plays for a benefit at La Mama, an experimental cafe-theatre that Ellen Stewart, a fashion designer, had opened in the East Village. We came up with a "conversation with herself" for Joyce Aaron, whom we knew as Sam Shepard's girlfriend and an actor in the Open Theatre. Joyce had made

us laugh talking about her "zippy" manner. This became an exchange between the "girlish" and "womanly" sides of her personality, culminating in an absurd mutual seduction. We called it *More! More! I Want More!* It is less than five minutes, more like three. A miniature sketch. Joyce performed it at La Mama, and it has been revived at least twice with other actors.

Lighting
A Funny Walk Home

The most valuable thing I learned in my two-plus years as an undergraduate at Yale was the basics of stage lighting. As a freshman I joined the Dramat, the undergraduate drama club. The university theatre, which the Dramat then shared with the Yale Drama School, was a traditional theatre with a proscenium stage and a balcony. Not wanting to act, I let myself be drafted onto the stage crew, learning how to build flats and helping to put up a set. The Dramat's lighting designer, a senior who needed to have a competent succession in place before he graduated, took two of us under his wing and systematically taught us the McCandless technique of lighting design. (The other boy, Gilbert Hemsley, went on to a wide-ranging career as a lighting designer and influential teacher-mentor of theatre technicians.)

Our first project was three student one-acts in the experimental theatre in the basement, where we set up the lights and hooked them up to the dimmers in the wings, big circular rheostats with individual wooden handles. I was enchanted by what I could do with these dimmers, the way light could make things appear and disappear, seem brilliant or dull, flat or three-dimensional, the way colors of light could intensify, clash, harmonize, dissolve into one another, the visceral effect on the viewer of the softness or abruptness of changes of color, direction, and intensity. Light theatricalizes space, energizes actors, dramatizes emotion. The rhythm, qualities, and dynamics of light shape the performance.

Later we worked on a science-fiction version of *The Tempest* in the big theatre upstairs. The conceit was that Prospero had a giant television screen of scrim through which he could view scenes in other parts of the island. I climbed enormous ladders to focus spotlights hung on swaying pipes suspended from the high grid and learned how to operate the old-fashioned dimmers in the wings. I stayed on in New Haven for an extra week after school ended to run the follow-spot for a show on alumni weekend.

Meanwhile I had managed to flunk math and philosophy. I made up the credits at Occidental College in Los Angeles in the summer and returned to Yale in the fall on probation, not permitted to participate in official extra-curricular programs. Nonetheless, I worked on setting up the lights for a production in one of the college dining halls of *Sweeney Agonistes* by T. S. Eliot and *Women of Trachis* by Ezra Pound. The plays were staged on platforms in the round. We fabricated the stage lights out of lengths of stovepipe. This was my introduction to modernism.

I redeemed myself academically that first semester, returned to the Dramat, and had the opportunity to design the lights for the big spring musical, a Sam Pottle original. I was thrilled to have access to so much equipment and used over a hundred instruments. The light booth in back of the balcony had recently been equipped with a large, hand-built, ten-preset dimmer console, the latest invention of George Izenour, a pioneer of electronic lighting control who was on the Yale faculty. This allowed me to make many elaborate cues, changing many lights all at once. I had taken Bauhaus artist Josef Albers's course in color and used double sets of area lights in the beams, not just pink and blue but lavender and green as well. For a dance number I punctuated a turquoise wash with big pools of blazing orange. A senior electrician ran the show, cued by the stage manager, with his assistant setting up cues ahead of him, while I sat in the audience and watched.

I would embrace every opportunity to do theatre lighting from then on, although it was never my main work.

A decade later, in the mid-1960s, I lived for several years on Cornelia Street in Greenwich Village with John P. Dodd, the waiter and light man at the Caffè Cino, as he gradually became a serious lighting designer with a wide-ranging career. In the beginning I helped him set up any number of shows. The lights were heavy, the light pipes high and hard to reach, the power cords stiff and dirty. We often worked through the night, the only time the stage would be available to us, setting up shows at Caffè Cino, La Mama, Judson Memorial Church, and small theatres all over the city. Several times Johnny left me running the lights for the performances while he went on to another project. I enjoyed watching shows from the light booth, my hands on the controls, feeling like the invisible magician making the illusions appear. Johnny's wildly expressive ideas about lighting had me dancing with the dimmers. This was before electronic dimmer boards, when lighting control was much more physical.

In 1967, with Johnny away on tour with La Mama Troupe, I

designed and ran the lights at the Caffè Cino for *A Funny Walk Home*, an unforgettably powerful play by Jeff Weiss, who also starred in it and made a tremendous impression. Jeff played a young man coming home from a mental hospital, his mania far from cured. At the climax he stopped the action and forced the audience to vote on whether he should end the play before he murdered his parents or go ahead and do it. Most audiences, chillingly, urged him to go on. Jeff was an extraordinary actor and made the story horrifyingly real. I lit the play harshly but ended it tenderly, after the ghastly dénouement, with a slow, lyrical fade-out on teenage George Harris III as the innocent younger brother. Years later it came out that I had ignored and infuriated the director of *A Funny Walk Home*, Jeff's partner Ricardo Martinez, who was still mad at me. In truth I had hardly noticed him. I was too dazzled by Jeff, who channeled a uniquely brilliant, terrifying energy riding the ragged edge between fiction and reality.

Vorspiel nach Marienstein

Johnny and I wrote another tiny playlet with another friend, Ondine (Robert Olivo), the opera queen, actor, speed freak, Warhol star, and irrepressible wit, at an intimate all-night party in an apartment off upper Fifth Avenue. I had a job proofreading *The Village Voice* every week at the printing plant in Newark, New Jersey, so it was 3 a.m. by the time I arrived. The others had taken LSD earlier in the evening. I sniffed crystal amphetamine to catch up. Johnny, Ondine, and I (as scribe) amused ourselves by writing a play about a brief, ecstatic imaginary encounter between two of our favorite monsters, Richard Wagner and

Ludwig II of Bavaria. On a previous acid trip Johnny and I had visited Ludwig's splendiferous castles, including Linderhof, which features an artificial grotto complete with lake and swan boat, built for a private performance of *Lohengrin*. We wrote simultaneous, wildly romantic monologues for the two raving, larger-than-life characters, culminating in the appearance of a hysterically screaming Kundry (from *Parsifal*), a kiss under a waterfall, and a declaration that "Kisses are the language of love." I titled it *Vorspiel nach Marienstein*.

Our dear friend Joe Cino was also at the party, in despair and having a panic attack that turned out to presage his suicide two weeks later. Our cenacle of friends and peers was devastated by his death, but the Caffè Cino continued operating.

Later that spring *Vorspiel nach Marienstein* was performed at the Cino on a program I threw together to replace my production of Søren Agenoux's play *Donovan's Johnson*, which had self-destructed and closed a week early (see below). Ondine was perfectly cast as Wagner, with Charles Stanley posing as Ludwig and dancer Deborah Lee as Kundry. Magie Dominic made a tinsel waterfall that fell out of a box on the ceiling on cue for the final moment.

The play is silly and shallow. Its existence reflects the authors' unwarranted assumption that anything we did was great because we were the ones doing it, and we were unique and great. The writing may have a certain glittery dazzle, but the goings-on are nonsensical and not funny or outrageous unless you are a member of the gay cult of Wagner and Ludwig. The idea that these two were romantically attracted to each other is nothing but wishful thinking, as far as I know.

In the little play's favor, it reminds us that one of the freedoms we espoused in our youth, and acted out at the Caffè Cino, was the freedom to be frivolous and silly. I still treasure it.

Directing/presenting
Chas. Dickens's Christmas Carol, Donovan's Johnson, With Creatures Make My Way, Vorspiel nach Marienstein, Sundance Festival, The Life of Juanita Castro, Dr. Kheal, Hurricane of the Eye

Søren Agenoux (né Frank Hansen) floated into my life in 1962. A sui generis writer and charmer, Søren many nights crashed on the sofa in Johnny Dodd's and my tiny apartment on Cornelia Street. Søren and I had a lot of fun together. He introduced me to pornography and amphetamine, among other sleazy delights, supplying me with fuzzy Xeroxes of dirty stories, long before porn was readily available, and little aluminum-foil packets of the glittery powder. Sniffing amphetamine or swallowing related pills allowed us to stay up all night and write twice as much as we would have otherwise. Søren reviewed John Rechy's ground-breaking novel *City of Night* for me when I was an editor at *The Village Voice;* but he was too far-out for *The Voice*, and that was his sole appearance in its pages. He worked for the arts program at Judson Memorial Church in the early 1960s, publishing nine issues of an idiosyncratic zine, *The Sinking Bear*, on the church's Gestetner mimeograph machine. He had a disastrous habit of criminality and made enemies on both coasts by ripping people off. He forged checks, was arrested, and spent much of 1965 in prison on Rikers Island.

Søren was a good friend whose very existence seemed to me peculiarly provisional. He didn't mean things the way other people did, carrying irony to another, transcendent level. I accepted his writing without thinking I needed to understand it. Amphetamine was surely a factor in its brilliance. There was a lightness about it that I appreciated, though I may have been imagining that, and a febrile intensity: he was serious, although the result was apparently camp. So I was thrilled to have the opportunity to direct his play *Chas. Dickens's Christmas Carol* at the Caffè Cino in December 1966. By now I was well established as a critic, but I wanted to direct as much as ever and embraced the challenge of making Søren's far-ranging images actually happen in the confines of that narrow room crowded with tables and chairs. Believing anything was possible, Joe Cino egged us on.

Our cast was rich in personality. Ondine brought his notorious sardonic wit to the role of Scrooge, which seemed (probably was) made to order for him. Charles Stanley, one of my best friends, played Tiny Tim on his knees, with a child's crutch. Søren's sweet boyfriend Arnold Horton was an earnest Bob Cratchitt. Søren himself in a frilly dress and bonnet played Mrs. Cratchitt. Donald L. Brooks, an innovative director, was alarmingly sepulchral as Marley's Ghost, and Jacque-Lynn Colton, a member of La Mama Troupe inspired by European training, embodied Christmas Past with a crown of flaming candles on her head, the token woman. Johnny's inventive lighting isolated different areas for the different times and locales, including a helicopter tour of the Dismal Swamp, a metaphor for Vietnam. Søren's deranged-sounding script deconstructed the familiar story in a highly suggestive if incoherent way. We all felt we were part of something special.

Ondine, and by extension the "Warhol crowd," is said to have brought speed into the Cino, but I'm sure it was already there. Amphetamine amplified the craziness we were caught up in and living through. It was a terrible moment, when the idealistic radical freedom of the early sixties was breaking down into chaos and self-destruction, of which Joe Cino's grisly suicide a couple of months later would be an unmistakable portent.

I directed a second play by Søren Agenoux, *Donovan's Johnson*, in the spring of 1968 at the Caffè Cino, which continued to present plays for a year after Joe's death. It was a desperate time for me personally, and Søren's script was very dark. The characters were two bitter ex-cons released from Sing Sing and stranded in Ossining, New York, where a sweet-natured small-town youth (played by Arnold) tried to help them. The surreal second scene had the two men sweeping an imaginary stone up and down the center aisle of the cafe in moonlight, reciting the stage directions to Verdi's *La Forza del Destino* over fragments of Beethoven's "Moonlight" Sonata. The play didn't make any sense, especially with the principal actors wacked out on contradictory drugs, and the run turned into an hallucinatory nightmare. Arnold left town, and Charles Stanley, who was now managing the Cino, mercifully closed down *Donovan's Johnson* a week early.

To fill the resulting gap in the Cino schedule, I directed Charles in a revival of H. M. Koutoukas's *With Creatures Make My Way*. "Directed" is not quite the right word, as Charles declined to do anything I suggested, conspiring with Harry to offer his own interpretation, which I accepted with as good grace as I could muster. We also threw together a production of *Vorspiel nach Marienstein*, as described above, and Rev. Al Carmines came over from Judson Church to sing some of his wonderful songs, accompanying himself on a tiny harpsichord.

Søren wrote a third play, *Donovan's Brain*, which took on the megalomaniac transportation czar Robert Moses, indubitably a great subject. He wanted me to direct it at Judson Church, which could have been arranged. We pulled together a private reading at Judson, with possible actors in the parts, including Ondine as Moses. Unfortunately the writing was so convoluted and self-referential that I couldn't make head or tail of it, imagine how to make it presentable to an audience, or face wrestling with its many problems, not sure I had sufficient energy or presence of mind. Right or wrong, I hated the play's bitter tone and finally said I couldn't and wouldn't direct it. This was a heavy blow to Søren, who seems to have needed me to take his plays from page to stage. *Donovan's Brain* was never produced, and that was the end of Søren's playwriting career.

For three summers, 1966-68, I ran a festival theatre in Bucks County, Pennsylvania, called Sundance. Wolfgang Zuckermann, the harpsichord-kit maker, had built the little open-air amphitheatre in 1963 with his friend Eric Britton as a venue for chamber music, with names of great composers lettered in gold across the proscenium. Eric moved to Paris, and responding to a column I wrote about doing theatre in the country, Wolfgang offered to sell Sundance to me. This was a laughable idea as I had no money. Instead I persuaded him to hire me as manager and radically expand the programming.

The time was right, everybody was availabe and affordable, and Sundance presented an extraordinary smorgasbord of contemporary theatre, dance, poetry, and music, bringing theatre companies from New York including La Mama Troupe, Judson Poets' Theatre, and the Open Theatre, dancers and choreographers including James Waring, Remy Charlip, Robert Schwartz, Beverly Schmidt, and Aileen Passloff, poets Allen Ginsburg and Peter Orlovsky, far-out musicians including La Monte Young, Terry Riley, Cecil Taylor, and Ravi Shankar—in addition to first-class chamber music and recitals by the likes of Ralph Kirkpatrick and Fernando Valenti. Every year Wolfgang curated an evening of experimental films. Johnny came to do the lights the first summer but was otherwise occupied after that. I got to live in the country all summer, with amazing artists coming through. We had a tennis court, a swimming pool in the woods where we could swim naked, and a theatre where we could do anything we liked!

My mother's younger brother, Alfred Brooks, and his wife, Maxine Munt, were modern dancers and choreographers in New York beginning in the late 1930s. Al and Max played a crucial role in my life as mentors, exemplars of the artist life, generous, loving familial friends, and later as producers of my plays. After a year of ballet classes with Nina Fonaroff as part of the Stella Adler curriculum, I took modern dance classes with Al and Max regularly for several years in their studio at Forty-Third and Sixth Avenue, which helped my posture and sense of the body in space, although I never got good enough to dance with their company. They often had me over to dinner and encouraged me to play Al's piano at times when I had no piano of my own. My father thought they were a bad influence on me, and from his point of view they were. They never made money as artists; Maxine was chair of the dance department at  Adelphi University and the dance critic for *Show Business*, and Al sometimes worked as an office temp to fill the gaps. They believed, as I still do, that the artist's life is glorious and to a great extent its own reward, not to be measured in dollars.

In the mid-1960s Al and Max's loft building gave way to an office tower. Priced out of New York, they relocated to Denver, where they rented two floors of a small downtown building and opened a dance studio and a small theatre they called The Changing Scene. Inspired by the idealistic, experimental, art-for-art's-sake energy they had seen develop in downtown New York, Al and Max dedicated the Changing Scene to "new works in all media." Heroically, they would sustain the

Changing Scene for thirty years, encouraging the work of countless young artists.

In the crazy summer of 1968, they invited me to come put on a show. That was the last season of Sundance: Wolfgang was selling the property and moving to England. I was sick of living in New York and trading on my personal opinions of plays good and bad. My own theatrical career was going nowhere, and I was dizzy from drugs and the ups and downs of the sixties, turned on, tuned in, ready to drop out. Abandoning my position at *The Village Voice*, in late August I drove across the country with Johnny Dodd in my Thunderbird convertible, following the chaos of the Chicago Democratic convention on the radio. My destination was San Francisco, where our poet friend Diane di Prima had rented a house in the Haight and was practicing zen meditation with Suzuki Roshi, which sounded like just what I needed. On the way west, we stopped off in Denver and put together a three-part theatrical event at The Changing Scene.

To open the program, Johnny devised a performance piece he called *Political Sonata Vision*, combining dance, projections, lighting effects, and declamation of texts by e. e. cummings, Aristotle, Hitler, and Thomas Paine.

I followed with a production of *Dr. Kheal*, a short play by María Irene Fornés, a Cuban-American playwright I knew from the Open Theatre and Judson Church. The play is a monologue in the form of a lecture by an increasingly addled professor, who projects an air of bemused, off-beat, ambiguous wisdom, a tone unique to Irene. I loved its elusive charm. Bob Breuler, an actor friend of Al's, played the part.

Finally, Johnny gamely donned a black lace dress to act the title character in Ronald Tavel's absurdist docudrama *The Life of Juanita Castro,* originally written as a screenplay for an Andy

Warhol film. Warhol's non-actors lacked the patience or presence of mind to learn lines, and Andy wasn't interested in rehearsals; so Ron cleverly provided an onstage Director who tells the formally posed actors what to say and do, line by line. This was the dawn of modern cross-gender theatrics; having Johnny play Juanita was a tribute to Charles Stanley's unforgettable *Medea* at the Caffè Cino. I cast three of Al and Max's female dance students as Fidel, Raul, and Che Guevara, wearing boots and beards and smoking cigars, and I played the Director. Irresistible in its peculiar ridiculousness, *The Life of Juanita Castro* suited the intimacy of the Changing Scene. Andy had taken Ronnie to dinner with Fidel Castro's brother-in-law, and I only much later realized how cunningly the movie they made together replicates the upper-class exile milieu. My interpretation distanced itself more archly and naively. What I related to about Ron's play was its style. The same with Irene's bagatelle. Were they merely silly? The world was falling apart; was this my best stab at not giving in to utter dismay? I had said anything I had to "say" in years of essays for *The Village Voice*. Working in the theatre I wanted to play, to make something happen that audiences would be tickled and stimulated by without having their taste and intelligence insulted.

Six months of Zen and Diane's macrobiotic diet cured me of my amphetamine habit. I built myself a clavichord and wrote a journal shaped by the *I Ching*. My Zen practice climaxed in an all-day meditation (*sesshin*) and a weekend at Tassajara, the mountain monastery. My car gave out. I was increasingly broke. Theatre seemed irrelevant in the hippie kingdom, where everyday life was theatre. I had lunch with Judith Malina when the Living Theatre came to the Bay Area on a national tour. Their non-violent brand of revolutionary anarchism was aggressively rejected by the Berkeley hotheads, and she was broken-hearted.

Johnny, who had gone back to New York after our show in Denver, came to California to act with La Mama Troupe in Tom O'Horgan's movie of *Futz*. Having failed utterly to connect with the theatre world of San Francisco or make myself a sustainable life there, I went back with him. He put me to work running the lights for a rock musical on Bleecker Street, *Earthlight*, and I slowly eased back into the whirl, trying to hang onto my Buddhism. I had expected that all systems were about to dissolve into formless bliss or break down into chaos—and then they didn't, it all mostly just went on, as bad or worse but not stopping. I didn't want to go back to reviewing. But I had to do something, and theatre was all I knew.

Emanuel Peluso and Lucy Silvay, a playwright-actor couple, were especially good friends to me in this confused and difficult but still somewhat exalted time, making me welcome in their cozy studio glittering with colorful scarves and acrylic artifacts on Bethune Street in what was then the remote West Village. They were high on yoga and Arica, marijuana was $15 an ounce, and we tripped together on LSD. I had liked Manny's first play, and he asked me to direct his new one, with Lucy in a prominent role. The title, *Hurricane of the Eye*, emerged in a taxi on the way to La Mama.

The play was softcore Pinteresque, vaguely ominous, charming, rather dry—at least that's all I managed to see in it. I arranged a poised, classical production with painted clouds on the walls ala Magritte. Johnny designed the lights, and we devised a unique effect to begin the

play and separate the scenes: in place of a black-out, we invented the red-out, the stage and entire theatre flooded with red light before and between scenes—conceptual darkness.

Captain Jack's Revenge

Johnny's fascination with Native Americans led me to the story of Captain Jack and the Modoc War of 1873. I was slowly waking up to the reality and inexorable near-erasure of the Native Americans. It was late in the game when the Modocs, one of the last free tribes, were removed from their homeland near the California-Oregon border and set down on a reservation among the Klamaths, their traditional enemies. Kintpuash—called "Captain Jack" by his American friends in Yreka—twice led his people back home to Lost River. When the cavalry tried to move them to the Klamath reservation for the third time, shots were fired, and the Modocs retreated into the nearby lava beds (now a national monument and worth a visit). For six months they held off increasingly larger forces of the U.S. Army, killing dozens of American soldiers. Finally, at a peace conference, Jack pulled a revolver and shot General Canby dead, imagining that would be the end of it. Instead the Army sent 1,000 reinforcements and he was hanged.

The utter hopelessness of this story struck a chord in me a century later, when the Vietnam War was dragging on, the country was tearing itself apart, and I had lost any sense of direction in my own life. I identified with Jack's bravery and despair.

The "reality" level of my play posited a hip, alienated contemporary couple, Mary and Jack, hanging out and playing with art in their bohemian loft (not unlike Manny and Lucy, or Johnny and me). William, a young draft dodger, is staying with them, preparing to flee to Canada. Mary's father, an army general, comes for an unexpected visit, and they entertain themselves by acting out a documentary play Jack is writing about Captain Jack's dramatic downfall. (I have an irrepressible fondness for the play-within-a-play. My last play, *Hamlet in Love*, has two!)

The opening scene was a collage of media, piling on television, music, slides, film, telephones, the doorbell, and a siren in the street outside—the texture of everyday city life. Copying an effect from Bob Heide's *Moon* (not consciously realizing it at the time), I had the actors listen to an entire track of an LP without speaking or moving—George Harrison's "While My Guitar Gently Weeps," from the Beatles' white album, a cry of compassion to set the emotional tone. For the play's historic reenactment scenes, the staging by contrast was plain and bare, a drummer keeping an ominous beat. Then I wove the two modes together before the stark, senselessly tragic ending.

Ellen Stewart gave me a date to present *Captain Jack's*

Revenge at La Mama in April 1970. She snagged me a smart, up-and-coming director who liked my modern couple and wanted me to write more of their story, suggesting I reduce or eliminate the historic parts of the play. He could probably have helped me to make it "work" better, but I wanted to see the play I had written this time, well aware how clumsy and far-fetched it was, imagining that was part of its charm. Directing one's own play was more or less taboo, but I was a director first and knew what I wanted to see. Making up the play, I had tried to imagine not just the fictional reality I was proposing but also the presentation of it on a stage, consciously creating a theatrical event as well as telling a story. So I wound up directing *Captain Jack's Revenge* myself. I knew the space in Ellen's new theatre on East Fourth Street, bare brick walls and raked seating with a center aisle, and knew how I wanted to use it. I conceptualized the lighting the play needed, and Johnny's protégé Steve Whitson realized it for me. I cast Ondine and Lucy Silvay as Jack and Mary and the director/personality John Vaccaro as the hapless Reverend Eleazar Thomas.

I never know what the audience sees, what comes across, what anyone imagines to be my purpose, whether the magic happens for them or they are just being politic or kind. Most people don't say much, or anything specific, and I am usually too caught up in my own fraught reflections to hear what they do say. Arthur Sainer wrote an elegant appreciation of *Captain Jack's Revenge* in *The Village Voice*. Bill Hoffman called it "the first seventies play" and dibsed it for his new anthology. There must have been applause after the performances, although the play was intended to leave people flabbergasted.

Its fierce ambiguity reflected my sense of history and life in general. The modernist reality of present-day domestic comedy deberately jarred with the garage-theatre crudeness of the Captain Jack scenes, largely transcripts from the historical record. What were we to make of Jack's predatory sexual come-on to young William? And the ending had a crazy twist. As Jack climbs the gallows to be hanged for murdering the American general, a shot rings out from behind the audience and he falls dead, shot in the back. (I imagined Olivier doing this fall.) The moment has an eerie resonance.

The play reflected my personal reality too. I myself was half a romantic couple, both of us caught up in our own ambitions and obsessions, which pulled us apart as much as they connected us. I too was grappling with an ambiguous sexuality and loss of illusions. Growing up in the Middle West in the 1940s, I had been programmed with a privileged Pollyanna outlook—everything is working out for the best—that evidently is not always the case.

I worked incredibly hard on *Captain Jack's Revenge* and was proud of myself for making it happen. I had ambitions for this play and hoped it might "go someplace," that is, have a life beyond its limited run at La Mama. I tried to interest my old friend Helen Merrill, a thriving agent for playwrights, and she came to see it, but I don't think she liked it. (Ondine's acting was hard for some people to believe.) The play did get a little bit of attention, including a student production in upstate New York, which I went to see, and publication in German translation. Passing through London later that spring, I dropped off a script at the stage door of the Royal Court Theatre, and to my amazement, they produced it a year later, in their smaller upstairs space, under Nicolas Wright's direction. I wish I had been there to see it.

Act II

A Dog's Love

I wrote the one-act *A Dog's Love* in 1965, in the early days of my love affair with Johnny Dodd, when we were pushing the boundaries and puzzling out the ambiguities of coupledom. Set on the nonexistent boardwalk in Miami Beach, the play is a series of short scenes separated by sunsets and sunrises, intended as occasions for exuberant lighting effects. The story is whimsical and thin: Edsel, a bisexual opera director from New York, and his wife, Edna, pick up a pretty, complaisant beach boy and each have a little romance with him; then get back together and dump him with a wheelbarrowload of money.

A Dog's Love wanted an elaborate set and lighting and seemed too slight to be worth the effort. I had no confidence in it, and it languished unproduced until it occurred to me that it would work better as a chamber opera than a play. I sent the script to Al Carmines, who had written deliciously witty scores for similarly whimsical plays by Gertrude Stein, Irene Fornés, and Rosalyn Drexler. Al was busy with his own projects at Judson Church and passed it on to John Herbert McDowell, a composer and artistic personality well liked in downtown circles, who to my immense delight took it on. I loved John Herbert, a person of irrepressible creative spirit and good will. I had lit a concert he did at Judson including a piece for 100 dancers he choreographed to the Righteous Brothers' "You've Lost That Lovin' Feeling."

John Herbert set my language to distinctively angular music, the harmony dominated by seconds and sixths, the soprano, tenor, and baritone supported by a trio of oboe, cello, and harpsichord. I thought it was beautiful and gladly supplied a few more words where he needed them for the musical flow. John Herbert had a terrible time finishing the score. I remember agonizing afternoons at his loft on Fourteenth Street as he stalked around with no pants on, smoking cigarettes and drinking whiskey, putting off composing the final minutes. We had to postpone the opening for a week.

A Dog's Love premiered at La Mama in May 1971. John Herbert insisted on directing so he could cast his boyfriend, Eddie Barton, as the beach boy, Rod, and interpolate a gymnastic solo for him in the nude. My parents chanced to be in town and bravely came to the East Village to see my latest work. They must have assumed I was responsible for confonting them with

Eddie's cock, probably intending to offend, but it was not my idea—in fact I argued against it, much as I liked seeing naked guys on stage, thinking it distracted from the fantasy. I was glad not to direct *A Dog's Love* and had a better time playing harpsichord in the pit. Johnny and I had recently separated, and he didn't do the lights after all, sending us Beverly Emmons in his place, who did a fine job.

A Dog's Love is a weird parable. The plot suggests a flip, cynical spin on romance that is nothing like the way I actually felt. Rod is obviously a stand-in for Johnny, who was openly sexy avant la lettre and seven years my junior, both of us

more or less bisexual. It seems condescending to present him as a "dog"—a hustler, in fact, the pet and sexual plaything of the adults in the story—and cruel the way they reject him in the end. On the other hand, there is ecstatic transcendent beauty in these brief encounters, expressed in the gaudy lighting and wild harpsichord glissandos that accompany the oceanic off-stage sex. Edna and Edsel taste a freedom with Rod that is genuinely romantic, a revolutionary, unbounded dimension of love that empowers them to reconnect and go on, which is not negated but affirmed by the ironic ending. They value it so much they give him all their money.

Tony

Tony, a comic monologue in the form of an actor's acceptance speech at an awards ceremony, was inspired by watching on television as my actor friend Paul Sand accepted his Tony Award for *Story Theatre*. My script specifies red-lensed sunglasses like the ones Paul wore that night; I passed up a pair in a shop on Hollywood Boulevard, too broke at the time to buy them, and never did find any in New York. Acceptance speeches are a legitimate if obvious target for mockery, and I let myself go, the overexcited actor giddily rambling off into a stream-of-consciousness reliving of a love affair with a one-legged woman, complete with orgasm, and a flip-out right there on the podium. It was either perverse black humor or extremely bad taste—both, I daresay.

Although the part is written for a man, Lucy Silvay played it brilliantly at La Mama, where *Tony* served as a kind of dessert after *A Dog's Love* so audiences didn't go away hungry. The two plays had nothing to do with each other beyond sharing an alarmed, alienated outlook and ironic metatheatrical sensibility that might be seen as my own emerging style.

In at least two later renditions of *Tony* in other settings, the actor was pulled off the stage before reaching the end.

Peas

Uncle Al invited me do another production at the Changing Scene, and I wrote *Peas*. My Vietnam War play (think peace) depicted a "typical" American family going about their ordinary lives, Mother and Daughter shelling peas and chatting in the foreground, a folky duo of flute and guitar noodling along from the sidelines. They seem mellow and relaxed, but the tone of the play is weirdly haunted. Daughter keeps hearing unexplained noises. Father stumbles about mumbling to himself. Son is played by two actors, one a long-haired hippie, the other a soldier. The Mother keeps things on an even keel by denying that anything is wrong.

The experimentalism of *Peas*, encouraged by Al and Max's devotion to modern art, stretches realism to the breaking point. The play is more situation than story, but the mood is powerful. As the action develops, three  of the five actors start playing multiple characters, switching from one to another without notice, Daughter, for example, becoming her sweet Granny, her best friend Louise, and her own Mother. She is having some kind of unsatisfactory love affair with Jimmy, played by her Father. The mailman delivers a large, heavy wooden crate, which the Sons carry in and set up on trestles. The Father and Sons almost come to blows trying to pry it open. Granny distracts them with iced tea and memories. When no one is looking, the lid of the crate slowly rises and a wisp of smoke rises from it, the fragrance of incense filling the theatre. Everybody is freaked out without saying why. It is never acknowledged that the crate is the coffin of their soldier son.

The Denver actors were good-natured about doing anything I asked, however unnatural—unlike New York actors, who were often limited by preconceptions of their image as performers and resistant to contrary ideas. I long regarded *Peas* and the subsequent plays I did at The Changing Scene as my invisible masterpieces.

Directing
Eat Cake, XXXXX

Peas was too short to make an evening. Before heading west I had asked Jean-Claude van Itallie for a play to go with it. He gave me *Eat Cake*, a macabre two-character one-act about a woman being raped by materialism, the "rapist" forcing her to eat enormous quantities of cake. The play's punchy realism and in-your-face sociopolitical satire contrasted nicely with the melancholy dreaminess of *Peas*. Al found a bakery that gave us day-old cakes. The actors were gamely committed and made a huge mess that had to be cleaned up after every performance, something I tried to avoid in my own plays.

Immediately upon arriving in Denver to stage *Peas* and *Eat Cake*, I had met and tumbled into a love affair with Michele Hawley, a comely young artist who had been studying dance with Al and Maxine. With a woman in my life, I felt like a new man, profoundly refreshed. I wanted to stay in Denver, and Al and Max urged me to direct another production at the Changing Scene. So I followed up on *Peas* and *Eat Cake* with a play by William M. Hoffman that I had seen and liked at La Mama. I was forced to change Billy's title—*XXXXX*, with the Xs arranged in a particular pattern—because the ground floor of Al and Max's building was occupied by a theatre showing newly legalized sex films. (Gasps and moans from below were sometimes audible in quiet moments.) Xs inevitably suggested pornography, which was hardly Billy's intent. To be sure, the play opens with a naked man having a conversation with his penis, but there is nothing salacious about it. (The role was played by a lanky long-haired blond named Bert Kruse; I rehearsed him alone in front of the big mirrors in Al and Max's dance studio upstairs, both of us maintaining perfect poise.) Two members of the Vice Squad showed up one night to check us out; Al stalled them in the lobby until Bert had his pants back on. In fact, oddly given that Bill was Jewish, the play is a ritual invocation of the life of Jesus Christ: I presented it as

Jesus Play; it has also been done as *Nativity Play*. The author specified the music he wanted—several iterations of a chorale from Bach's "St. Matthew Passion" and Buffy Sainte-Marie singing "Until It's Time for You to Go"—gorgeous music for a gorgeous spectacle.

Country Music

After a productive and romantic two months in Denver, I continued west to Santa Barbara to pay a filial visit to my parents, not sure where I should be going next. If Michele and I hadn't broken up, I would have stayed in Denver. We had been looking for an apartment to share with her sister Tina when we went to see Nicolas Roeg's *Performance* and our idyllic harmony collapsed. Increasingly eager to be anywhere else but

New York, I had started building myself a cabin in the woods on Jean-Claude's beautiful, peaceful land outside Charlemont, Massachusetts, in the northern Berkshires. I thought I might go there. But fate intervened.

The previous spring, I had been invited to join the board of Theatre Genesis, the playwrights' theatre at historic St. Mark's Church in the East Village where I had seen Sam Shepard's first plays. This seemed like a ceremonial position and I had more or less forgotten about it. Finding me in Santa Barbara, a letter from Murray Mednick, another playwright on the board, informed me that the theatre's NEA grant had come through and I could have a slot in the 1971 season. I remembered Murray saying to me when I joined the Theatre Genesis board, "Now you have a theatre." This was what he meant. I immediately started writing a play. My Libra nature's struggle to balance city and country, east and west, gay and straight provided the themes.

Country Music is a dream play, plausibly all a dream in the mind of Boppo, an old man dozing in a rocker in the kitchen of his antiquated New England farmhouse. (Although bearing my grandfather's name, the character is nothing like him.) Two couples, one straight, one gay, fleeing the craziness of the city, come to spend the winter with Grampa. A stir-crazy neighbor (written for my friend Bill Hart) drops in for supper. Beethoven piano music is played offstage. The two gay men transform themselves into Mme. Ranevskaya and Trofimov and play a passionate scene from *The Cherry Orchard*. A baby girl wanders off into the woods and turns into a baby bear. Night falls. In the morning (Act II) it is spring, and the two couples, now much older, go back to the city, leaving Boppo alone with the bear, now full-grown, which transforms into the dream lover of his youth, played by my sweet friend John Albano.

Country Music is more like music than drama, a magic-realist fantasia on the life-matters that were foremost in my mind. I had given up on logic and rational causality in favor of instinct and intuition, but it really wasn't working out. My life had shrunk to what would fit into my VW. I was solitary, loveless, sleeping on my brother's sofa. I didn't have a job or want one. I was not happy living in the city but seemed to have no alternative.

There is a dreaminess and lyrical idealism to the play that counterbalances its sense of failure and despair. I had brilliant designers and a perfect cast for *Country Music* at Theatre Genesis, and it cast an unusual spell. The ending was marginally more cheerful than *Captain Jack's Revenge*, but the questions it raised remained open. I won an Obie Award for directing it, and Jerry Marcel was nominated for one for his exquisitely detailed set.

It was ironic that producing *Country Music* at Theatre Genesis drew me back to New York City once again. Needing a livelihood and a place to live, I taught a graduate playwriting class at Hunter College, resumed reviewing theatre for *The Village Voice*, and rented myself an apartment on East Fifth Street, a block from La Mama, giving the city another chance.

Directing
Bigfoot, Tango Palace

I could produce and direct other people's work at Theatre Genesis as well as stage my own plays. Ronald Tavel saw the opportunity and asked me to direct his new play *Bigfoot*. I had always liked Ron's work, drawn to his prickly intelligence and perversely eccentric sensibility. I had flirted with directing his jungle-movie extravaganza *Gorilla Queen* at Judson Church in 1967 but lost out to Larry Kornfeld, the principal resident director there. It was a kick doing *The Life of Juanita Castro* in Denver with Johnny. I published *Gorilla Queen* in my new anthology, *The Best of Off-Off-Broadway*, its image on the cover. (Many years later I would also publish, posthumously, Tavel's searing novel *Chain*.) Whatever the intentions behind Ron's work, I liked its scratchy energy.

Bigfoot was crazily ambitious, a wordy, difficult, sprawling play with a huge cast and elaborate sets and costumes, self-evidently straining the resources of our modest little theatre space above St. Mark's Church's parish hall. I never understood why Ron had such difficulty finding a more capable theatre to take on this extraordinary play—homophobia probably played a part. Our efforts to find a better situation for it, with or without me directing, came to naught so we squeezed it in.

The set features a monastery schoolroom on the right, with a stained glass window (later smashed) and a view of the cloister outside; on the left, a forest of giant redwoods; in the middle, a raised throne for Ronnie's brother, Harvey Tavel, later moved aside to reveal the stairway to heaven where Jacob wrestles with the angel. The square room was not wide enough to fit it all in.

Charles Terrel, the set designer, had the transformative idea of turning the play on the diagonal, which saved the day.

Directing is not a free creative art like playwriting. You have to work with what the playwright gives you, but that leaves plenty of room for interpretation. It takes tact, diplomacy, and steady will, if not necessarily a domineering personality, to persuade other people to fall in with your ideas, and this was especially true Off-Off-Broadway, where you were not backed up by the power of meaningful pay. At Theatre Genesis, as at the Cino and La Mama, directing meant producing as well, seeing to everything but the real estate and the money. I tried to give the playwright what he wanted and the play what it needed.

As with any production, there were endless practical tasks—auditions (which I dreaded) and casting, rehearsals five or six nights a week for five or six weeks, putting the play on its feet, getting everybody to learn their lines, having a set designed and built, costumes found and made, lighting

the play (myself from now on), arranging publicity. It all has to come together on opening night. For *Bigfoot*, the playwright was involved in every decision, occasionally taking charge, as when he insisted that I replace Lee Kissman with Walter Hadler in the leading role. (I still wonder what Lee would have made of it.) Everybody was paid the same amount, I think $100 a week. Admission was free.

With the stage taking up two-thirds of the room, *Bigfoot* crowded the audience into the corner. I'm not sure how well people liked it. There were many diverting theatrical effects and appealing actors, including two furry Bigfoots, played by the largest people I could find, and their small, furry, playful offspring, acted by twelve-year-old boys. There were meta-theatrical aspects including a beautiful light girl in a fake lighting booth who gets drawn into the dramatic action. If you bought into the fantasy reality of the play, it was great, in my opinion, but I could imagine being put off by the density of the language, confused by the overlapping modalities of the plot, dismayed by the mythic pretensions.

Bigfoot was a Pacific Northwest version of the Old Testament story of Jacob and Esau, weirdly doubled by the presence of Ronnie's actual brother. It must have made more sense on the theological level than I was prepared to realize: it led to the author's being appointed playwright-in-residence at the Yale Divinity School.

Irene Fornés, a writer and director of exquisite sensibility and force, felt as I did that the scrappy, do-it-yourself way of making theatre that had evolved in downtown New York was not an apprentice level or lesser spin-off of the big time but the thing itself. This was how we wanted to do theatre. On these makeshift stages we could do what we liked, say what we meant, materialize our actual visions, without being coopted into show business and serving commercial values we despised.

Cuban-born, Irene had lived in Paris for a time and been Susan Sontag's lover. Dan Wolf, the editor of *The Village Voice*, once remarked that Irene was the most intelligent person he had ever met. Her early play *Tango Palace* had been workshopped at the Actors Studio in 1964 but had not been publicly presented in New York. I arranged to direct a production at Theatre Genesis in January 1973.

Tango Palace was simple and short, with one small set and two actors, a welcome relief after *Bigfoot*. Irene, offering to help with the costumes, made a set out of bubblewrap she found on the street and largely took over the direction; I demoted myself to co-director. This was auteur theatre, and she was the auteur. We auditioned more than a hundred young men to play earnest, innocent Leopold. I wanted to cast a truly strange creature I had seen around the East Village as the androgynous Isidore. He was not necessarily an actor but would have embodied Isidore's gender ambiguity, which was what fascinated me about the play in the first place. Irene insisted on casting a skilled professional actor who was clearly a gay man. I thought there was a more interesting, less psychological story behind this poisonous gay pas de deux, the victimization of an innocent by an older, ruthless, manipulative queen.

Double Solitaire

Invited to come do another play at the Changing Scene, I revisited the characters from *Peas*, hoping to have the same actors play them. The next chapter in their lives involved two boy-girl couples confusedly switching partners. The mother and daughter who had been shelling peas now played double solitaire at a table that very slowly moved across the stage.

I arrived in Denver having written one act of what I conceived to be a "two-part" play, proposing to develop the second act in collaboration with the cast. It was a nerve-wracking way to work. Some nights we would have no ideas and feel hopeless; then at the next rehearsal something surprising would arise, and off we would go. The actors and designers liked having a more creative role than usual, and I was delighted with the whimsical, romantic, light-hearted result.

In this play I was talking to myself about how to live. The laid-back, homey, folksy style of my "ideal" family couldn't have been farther from the gay bohemian life I had been living in Greenwich Village, but I was clearly longing for it. Indeed, I was in the process of changing my life. I had come back to Denver hoping to reanimate my romance with Michele Hawley, now that we had had two years to think about it. The central question of the play became whether or not she would come back to New York with me. She did.

Prussian Suite

Ken Wollitz, an accomplished and lyrical recorder player I was privileged to play with for a time, introduced me to the story of Frederick the Great. Ken had a small German spinet harpsichord, and for a couple of years while I was living alone I went up to his apartment off the Bowery every week to sight-read early music with him. In early 1973 I moved to Brooklyn and built myself a harpsichord from a Zuckermann kit, which Ken and I inaugurated by giving a Sunday afternoon concert at an Upper West Side church, playing sonatas by Bach, Vivaldi, and Frederick the Great.

Yes, the warrior king of Prussia (1712-1786) was a flute player and composer. The pieces have a sparkling formality and charm typical of their post-Baroque moment. Playing his music with Ken led me to Frederick's life. I was especially interested in his youthful struggle with his father, Frederick William I. The sensitive crown prince was drawn to French culture and sensibility. The king, a bluff, bullying German, despised the French and their effeminate ways, demanding that his son man-up. Desperately unhappy, Frederick, accompanied by his adjutant and friend Captain Katte, ran away, seeking exile in France. The king's men apprehended them at the border, and Katte was beheaded in the courtyard outside Frederick's window.

My play about this story, *Prussian Suite*, was the next installment in my Oedipal cycle—also a representation of gay love and heartbreak, which I had been exploring for the past decade and was now leaving behind for good. I suppose it was irresponsible and frivolous of me to turn Frederick and Katte's friendship into a gushy bromance, but I was not trying to be a serious historian, and it made for a deliciously melodramatic plot. Frederick's sister Wilhelmina also figured in the story, a premature feminist pushed aside by her self-involved brother and practical-minded, heavy-handed father. I was intrigued with how the charming, fastidious prince turned into an aggressively militaristic ruler. The play concludes with the imagined death of the ailing king and Frederick's fatalistic acceptance of the weight of power (see *Henry IV, Part 2*).

The tragic story is told in fragments, the diction poised, pared down, elegant, allusive, reflecting the musical *style galant* that came into its own at Frederick's court. *Prussian Suite* was structured as chamber music: all but the first and last of the eleven short scenes were to be played twice, like dances in a baroque suite. Envisioning its being acted like chamber music, with a sensitive politesse among the players and mutual devotion to a unified performance, I brought Ken Wollitz to a rehearsal as a specialist in chamber music and asked him to help the actors get the idea. But it was hopeless. I had cast Ondine as the king, my multitalented friend Charles Stanley as the prince, and Jimmy Camicia of the Hot Peaches as Katte, three charismatic performers relying on ego and attitude to energize their presence, jockeying for domination or survival. I had to take what they had to give me.

For my Theatre Genesis production of *Prussian Suite* in January 1974, I designed an elegant symmetrical stage with a raked center section for the action, platforms at the sides for the musicians and idle actors. I lit the play entirely with candles—it took thirty to make it bright enough—and unblocked the tall arched windows so you could see the city lights outside, wanting the audience awake to being in New York in the 1970s as well as imagining Berlin in the 1730s. I backed the stage with a long decorative cloth I had brought back from Bali, black with gold figuration, which gleamed in the candlelight like a palace of the mind.

A key element was the evocative live music composed by John Smead, a talented guitarist from Chicago, which underscored every scene save one. The ensemble, seated cross-legged on one of the side platforms, consisted of Michele playing drone on a tamboura, John on guitar, and me on harpsichord, plus occasional recorders and sound effects including a tubular gong and a hatchet chopped into a tree stump.

The play is far too unclear. The prince is referred to throughout as the Rising Sun, Katte as Cat. If you didn't realize it was about Frederick the Great and already know the outlines of the story, it can't have made much sense. To make things more confusing, I had Charles and Jimmy switch roles for the repetitions of the scenes—a trick-too-far that I came to regret. I couldn't choose between them. I was intimidated by Ondine and Charles, who both indulged their egos outrageously, and Jimmy felt naked without glitter. I wanted the mise-en-scène to be stripped down and bare except for the red satin period jacket Frederick dons so the French will realize who he is.

I rehearsed *Prussian Suite* in my living room in Park Slope when I could persuade the actors to come to Brooklyn, which was then terra incognita to Manhattanites. Ondine understood the agony of the choleric king, plagued by gout and a resistant world. He was so brilliant and real in late rehearsals that I think he scared himself. Off amphetamine by now, he anesthetized himself with bourbon in the dressing room and never reached those heights in performance—which  was partly my fault: it was distractingly hard to control the king's antique wheelchair on the raked stage! Charles purred through his lines as the prince, practically singing them, an excessively precious performance, in my opinion, although it was my language that pushed him in that direction. I preferred Jimmy's rougher sincerity in the role, but the power dynamic flowed the other way and was impossible to fight. Georgia Lee, a Theatre Genesis regular, was ideally simple and touching as Wilhelmina.

Prussian Suite was an enchanting effect, an attempt to merge the visual poetry of Robert Wilson's stately stage works with dramatic character and narrative. I was much moved by the king's confrontation with Katte, a surrogate for his son, screaming, "Love me! Love me!" as he beats him with a riding crop; by the tragic love story; by Frederick's nobility as he yields to his fate and shoulders the burden of kingship.

A Wedding Party

Michele and I wanted to have a baby and decided we would get married, mainly for the benefit of our parents. We could stage the celebration at her family's house in Denver, although they were selling it and moving to New Mexico.

If I was going to be in Denver anyway, obviously I should write a new play and do it at the Changing Scene. Michele and I went up to my cabin at Charlemont, now finished and snug, and I wrote a short play called *The Dinner Show*, about a newly married couple hosting their first dinner party (see below). Realizing it was too surreal and ambiguous for such a straightforwardly happy occasion, I set it aside when we got back to Brooklyn and wrote another, more appropriate play, *A Wedding Party*, which we performed at the Changing Scene for two weekends in June 1974, just before our own wedding party. Again I arrived in Denver with a half-written play. We went up to a cabin in the Front Range so I could finish it, invigorated by the mountain air and thrilling romance of our commitment.

I used the play—or it used me—to explore and exorcize some of the complicated feelings I had at the prospect of being married. I was amazed, in love, light-hearted and entirely positive about it: it was what I really wanted to do. Still, getting married is a big step, with all kinds of practical and symbolic implications. I felt anxiety, fright, uncertainty, self-doubt, self-defense, irony—as well as sincere, genuine love for Michele and wide-open hope for the future.

Starting with the half-dozen characters I already had from *Peas* and *Double Solitaire*, I added a part for Michele as a

comical grandma (drawn from my own lovable Grammie, a paragon of positive thinking) and a wacked-out preacher who wanders in off the street for her to love. I sent my four couples into the mountains to sleep out among the trees and be married in the early morning.

In *A Wedding Party* the darkness is full of life and the suggestion of other dimensions. The rocks and picnic table glide into new positions in the night. Sleep-walkers appear, and spirits are at large. With a deal of sturm und drang, the play got the wonderful set it deserved, the stage transformed into a diorama of trees and sloping ground, framed in tree trunks and foliage, with a trio of musicians playing, humming, and twittering like birds on a platform up in the trees.

And then we actually did get married.

Cowgirl Ecstasy

With a family to support, I needed a steady income, and I wanted to be home at night. I was sick of reviewing plays, and I was not getting anywhere as a playwright and director in New York City, which, once glamorous, had now fallen on hard times, ever more decadent, dangerous, filthy, bankrupt, and falling apart. So I gave up on the theatrical scramble and embarked on an entirely new life chapter, married with child, going to work nine to five for David J. Way, successor to Wolfgang Zuckermann in the harpsichord-kit business, in Stonington, Connecticut, a seaside village halfway to Boston. I liked working with my hands and loved domesticity and regularity. The birth of my son Julian in January 1975 was one of the peak experiences of my life.

Michele and I hadn't entirely given up on theatre or a life in art. Our best friends in Stonington, Daniel and Melisande Potter, had a children's theatre company called the Mystic Paper Beasts, with which Michele and I both performed. Always a writer, I finished a long poem about Julian's gestation and birth (*American Baby*) and started thinking about a novel (*You Can Be You if I Can Be Me, Otherwise Trouble*).

Ironically, within a year of leaving New York, ditching the theatre world, and plunging into new life, I was selected for a $10,000 Rockefeller Foundation Award in Playwriting—unexpected recognition and the first real money I had ever made for writing plays. Uncle Al had recommended me for the grant, $1,500 of which would subsidize a production at the Changing Scene. So I was obliged to write another play. It was not easy to find time and space for writing, as any working writer-parent will recognize. I rented a chilly room downstairs from our apartment on Gold Street in Stonington and stole time from Michele and Julian all that winter to write *Cowgirl Ecstasy*.

As usual, the slippery thoughts and feelings I was privately wrestling with in the background of daily life came out in the play, embodied in a story very different from my own situation. *Cowgirl Ecstasy* portrays a rock band on tour, coming down in their hotel room after a performance, trying to be real with each other as they are being filmed for a documentary and spied on by the FBI. The band is falling apart. Tex Arcana, the lead singer, is sick of the road and gradually turning into J. S. Bach. The style is a kind of trashy magic realism much indebted, in my mind, to Sam Shepard's early work.

I eventually took a few weeks off from the harpsichord shop and staged a perfect production of *Cowgirl Ecstasy* in Denver in September 1976. The play bubbles with theatrical trickery as well as emotion and events. It calls for a cast of twelve plus a harpsichordist. An intrusive cameraman continuously tracks the action, a live video monitor at one side of the stage showing the actors in closeup, a mute sound person hovering over them with a boom mike. The FBI agent is represented by a lifesize pink satin doll dressed up in a suit and hat (ultimately depantsed), manipulated by a visible actor in black ala Bunraku. There is an adorable groupie and a poignant monologue by her father, who is dying of cancer from years of working with PVC, my geneticist friend Frank Lilly having challenged me to write about the malignant transformation.

I was reading Idries Shah's books on Sufism at the time, and the play is generously spiced with Sufi symbolism, including a palm tree crossing the stage. By the end the setting has opened up into a tropical island. I too had made my escape from show business, not unscathed, withdrawing to the idyllic parallel world of family and early music.

Cowgirl Ecstasy was produced in New York a year later by New York Theatre Strategy, a playwrights collective organized by Irene Fornés and actress-playwright Julie Bovasso. In 1973 I had declined their invitation to be a member, a decision I later regretted. But I was sick of my life in the city, alienated from the downtown theatre scene, struggling to move on and leave all that behind. So I kept my distance—although these were wonderful writers, the best of my peers, my own "family" of alternative artists, many of them friends, sharing my values as much as anyone did.

Ignoring my non-membership, Irene went ahead and scheduled an off-Broadway production of *Cowgirl Ecstasy*. Very much wanting my play to be seen by my peers in New York, I was thrilled. As it happened, though, Michele was pregnant again, and right at that moment we were in the act of moving to New Mexico, no time to lose. There was no way I could be in New York right then and direct *Cowgirl Ecstasy* myself. I approved a director I barely knew and hoped for the best.

It was a week before opening by the time I could break away. Irene arranged a Theatre Communications Group grant for me to fly back to New York and see what they had made of my play. The seventies was a time when directors had the upper hand, and this director had aggressively reconfigured my play. *Cowgirl Ecstasy* is about a rock band, but the only music we hear in it is Bach harpsichord music—that's the joke. He turned it into a rock musical, using some of my dialogue as lyrics, placing the band downstage, backgrounding the action of the actual play. My imaginative, witty use of live video was reduced to a hapless actor wandering around with a Bolex pretending to shoot film. The addition of songs made the play much longer, forcing a second intermission, destroying my two-act form, and it was too late for me to do anything about it. It was a travesty, a gross misrepresentation of my beautiful, funny play and a complete fiasco, one of the most miserable experiences of my life.

Act III

<u>Directing</u>

Krapp's Last Tape and *The Zoo Story, West Side Story, Life Is Dream*

In spring 1977, I quit my job at the harpsichord factory, and Michele and I rashly moved from Stonington, Connecticut, to Taos, New Mexico, following her parents and five siblings. Our second son, Alfred, was born at home in Taos that October, an occasion of incomparable joy. It would be a challenge to support us in what turned out to be one of the poorest counties in the country. On the other hand, it was gloriously beautiful, a visceral thrill just to be there—higher vibes, wider, emptier horizons. Eastern Connecticut had been something of a cultural black hole, the economy dominated by war industries. In the wild, wide open west, there was more creative energy on the loose.

There turned out to be an unexpectedly lively theatre scene in Taos. Michele and I saw a production by the Taos Theatre Company. I liked it so much that I called up the co-founder of the company, Bill Bolender, whose acting I had found riveting. He came right over and we clicked immediately: he said I could direct all their plays. He wanted to do *Krapp's Last Tape* by Samuel Beckett on a double bill with *The Zoo Story* by Edward Albee, a classic off-Broadway pairing. Good idea! Bill and Steve Parks, his Taos Theatre Company partner, were ideal casting for Albee's archetypal characters, and Krapp would be a splendid role for Bill.

Beckett is one of the great writers of my time, and I welcomed the opportunity to direct *Krapp's Last Tape*. I love Beckett's writing. His plays are notoriously bleak but he is also uniquely funny in his bone-dry way, *Krapp's Last Tape* the most openly tender of his major plays.

The shallow stage in front of the movie screen of the subterranean Plaza Theatre was well suited to these small-scale, intimate plays. Bill and Steve and I got along fine, although I'm not sure I did much actual directing. They had definite ideas about what they wanted to do, and I tried to help. Putting on a play is a matter of energy, intention, logistics, and, above all, showing up; we were experienced enough to know what it takes and how to enjoy the process.

There is a snarky tone to *The Zoo Story* that I don't altogether like—it is too calculated, too much of a setup. I like Albee's smart writing but resent being drawn into collusion with his bleak judgment of humankind. Bill and Steve did a fine rendition of Albee's little death-duet. Bill was a juicy Krapp—how he relished the banana!—not necessarily what I would have expected or directed but wonderful on its own terms..

Bill Whaley, the owner of the Plaza Theatre and a leading arts businessman in Taos, had the idea of producing *West Side Story* at the Taos Community Auditorium. On the strength of the Beckett-Albee, he hired me to direct it for a fee of $500, which I sorely needed. *West Side Story* is a

Gesamtkunstwerk, a masterwork of total theatre (although the book is somewhat lame). I remembered the original Broadway production with its beautiful set by Oliver Smith and lighting by Jean Rosenthal and took on the project as homage to the original director-choreographer, Jerome Robbins, a theatrical wizard if not, apparently, a nice man: Leonard Bernstein and Arthur Laurents were not speaking to him by the time their show opened in 1957.

West Side Story's combative ethnic gangs in 1950s New York offered equal recognition to the contrasting Spanish and Anglo communities in Taos. Bill put together a team to do the show, which had a cast of thirty-eight. There were two choreographers, one for each gang, a music director to work with the singers on the songs, a conductor to lead the orchestra in the pit. I directed the actors and figured out how to make the show work on the bare-bones stage with limited scenery. Musicals were what drew me to theatre in the first place so I was intrigued by the conceptual problem. Lighting did much of the directing for me, light changes structuring the action, defining locales and atmosphere, making the show look theatrical, helping to tell the story. The community auditorium's inadequate dimmer board kept breaking down. My assistant director, a member of a local Lesbian theatre troupe, was highly critical of my directing. She thought I should be teaching people to act, holding improv workshops and the like, and organized her own counter-rehearsals behind my back. We survived on grapefruits to keep ourselves healthy in the Taos winter. Somehow it all worked out, and the show was a huge hit. The novelist John Nichols wrote a rave review in *The Taos News*. I have never had such a success before or since.

Julian was three, and Alfred was a baby. I hated being away from home every evening and didn't really mind when Michele asked me not to direct any more plays for a while. I had a part-time job as tech director at the auditorium, wrote the arts page for the *Taos News*, tilled a vegetable garden for Michele, baked bread, built a beautiful harpsichord for a slippery couple in Santa Fe, helped Bill Bolender build a dome house in Talpa, lit *Fiddler on the Roof*, and struggled to keep us afloat.

In the course of my usual random reading, I chanced upon *La Vida Es Sueño*, one of the great classics of the Spanish Golden Age, and was hooked. Pedro Calderón de la Barca's famous play is a fearsome, fantastic tale of a father misunderstanding and mistreating his son. The existing translations were impossibly stilted. In order to read it more closely, I found myself writing out a "new English version." I don't know Spanish, but I had several translations at hand and went back to the dictionary when in doubt about what Calderón was saying, and I know Shakespeare, his contemporary. It was thrilling to write in the voice of a master, conniving in a high poetic melodrama, letting the language be as musical, grandiose, intricate, and fanciful as I liked. It was a refreshing break from contemporary realism:

this had nothing to do with ordinary life. I was writing lines for royalty, heightened beings speaking a heightened language.

There was a great role in it for Bill Bolender as Segismundo, the tragically wronged prince who sets his foot on his father's head before he finally forgives him, and a sweet role for Steve Parks as a foppish prince. The Taos Theatre Company would produce it in January 1979 at the Taos Community Auditorium.

Bill persuaded a famous artist, Larry Bell, to design our set. I went over to Larry's hacienda to discuss it. The sprawling stage of the community auditorium was all wrong for this play, threatening to dissipate its energy, and I was struggling to conceptualize a compressed "empty" space thrust forward toward the audience. Distracting me with a taste of cocaine, Larry didn't take much interest in my ideas. He wanted to see what would happen if he put large sheets of heavy paper into the high-tech furnace he used to fuse metallic molecules onto glass, producing the miraculous graduated-mirror structures that are his claim to fame. Bill and Steve constructed a sprawling "castle" of ramps and platforms and stapled Larry's coated paper onto the face of it. I couldn't find any good way to light it; from a distance it just looked gray.

Using the space that way turned my vision of fierce dramatic intensity into conventional historical melodrama, and Bill's acting went in the same direction. Segismundo, raised like a caged beast, has turned into a monster; Bill had a dentist friend make him a fang. Having no choice, I got into the spirit and had a good time with the comic characters who relieve the darkness of the underlying story. Michele's father, Dr. Hawley, played the king with a fine bedside manner. Michele played Rosaura, the female lead, who arrives in Poland disguised as a man. (I was quite enamored of this image.) My pal Jonathan

Gordon, a stand-out as Schrank in *West Side Story*, was her sidekick, Honker. Right at the start of the play, Michele had to deliver a monologue that went on for three pages. Bill lolled on a rock with his back to the audience and made faces at her. I loved her in the role, but her squabbles with the other women in the company followed us home and made me swear never to direct her in a play again.

My composer friend Peter Hartman came from San Francisco to do music for the production and raised the whole level of the production, also turning on the wall furnace in our poorly insulated house, which we had been struggling to warm with wet wood. That cheered me up. Taos can be tough in winter, and in many ways *Life Is Dream* was a nightmare. It is a glorious work, and I was happy to be doing it, but we were perilously broke, and it did nothing to improve our situation. In retrospect, putting on a Spanish classic in English translation in a majority Spanish-speaking community was wrong-headed from the get-go. Years later Irene Fornés directed a brilliant bilingual production of *La Vida Es Sueño* at INTAR in New York that was stark and fierce like what I'd had in mind and didn't have the cojones to make happen.

Heavy Pockets

I gave up trying to make a living in Taos, called David Way in Stonington, humbled myself, and went back to my old job at the harpsichord works. Driving away from Stonington two years earlier, we hoped we would never see the place again, but it was a relief to be back. It would be six years before I directed another play. I hunkered down to making the best of small-town family life and a steady job producing instruments of beauty. I had my cabin at Charlemont to get away to from time to time, with and without the family. Michele applied herself to becoming a skilled harpsichord decorator. I loved being her husband and partner and father to my growing sons.

There was no way I could direct plays, but nothing would stop me from writing them. *Heavy Pockets*, written in 1980, is a comedy drawn from my theatrical adventures in Taos, an affectionate mockery of my friends and myself for our pretensions to doing more than scrape along. Thinly veiled versions of Bill Bolender, Steve Parks, me, and our three wives are caught up in staging (you guessed it) *Life Is Dream* at the community auditorium. Meanwhile an eccentric Englishman is in town organizing a D. H. Lawrence festival, for which Steve Parks's character is writing a play about Lawrence. What with a rival Lesbian theatre company, a murder 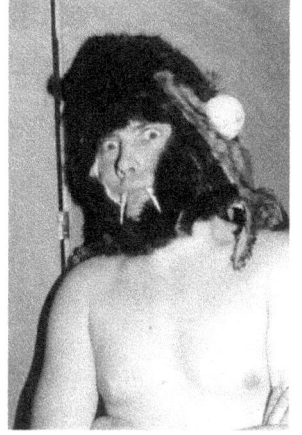 that may be imaginary, and a dancing policeman, it's quite an affair. I didn't have time to go to New York or Denver to put it on, so I dispensed with considering the limitations of my usual venues—La Mama, Theatre Genesis, The Changing Scene— and wrote it for a real theatre, with three real sets for the three acts. As a result, perhaps, it has never been seen, apart from a staged reading in our living room theatre in Westerly, Rhode Island, in 1983.

That was great fun. I conceptualized the dining room as the stage and put the audience in the living room, cobbled together a set with Michele's help, and mobilized a group of friends to play the characters script-in-hand. My painter friend Dennis Pinette was especially zesty in the Bolender role, and Robert Utter, a real actor, was lovely as the ghostly Brit. Julian, now eight, wanted to be part of it so I wrote him in as a second at the climactic duel. I was a little sorry I hadn't made my friends learn their lines, but that would have been too much to ask.

I have a special tender fondness for this play. I felt it was my breakthrough to the next level, tricky and playful and full of theatrical feeling. Performing it would be a tasty challenge for actors: many of them have double roles, playing broadly sketched secondary characters as well as their "real" parts. *Heavy Pockets* is not really about Taos but about marriage and the craziness of theatre, which I had loved and lost. I still wish someone would put it on.

Half Life

My title *Half Life* referred not to the fact that my life had turned into all work and no play (pun intended), but to Plato's idea that each of us is looking for his other half, seeking self-completion in a lover. I had been doing that myself, but *Half Life* is not about me. The principal characters are based on my close friends Joe Chaikin and Jean-Claude van Itallie, an actor-director and a playwright, though the events and issues of the play are freely abstracted from anything that really happened or was said and are, as the saying goes, entirely fictitious.

Joe and Jean-Claude had a transformative, highly productive love affair just about the same time I got together with Johnny Dodd in the early sixties, but they never gave in to each other to the extent of merging their lives. One thing they did well together was make theatre, collaborating with each other and the actors of the Open Theatre on *America Hurrah*, which Jean-Claude promoted into an off-Broadway hit that made him famous, and *The Serpent* (1968), a pioneering masterpiece of physical theatre. This is more or less the background to the situation at the beginning of *Half Life*, although all the facts are altered. Jean-Claude is Belgian-born; his fictional counterpart, Saïd, is Persian. The plot about Saïd's unrealized union with Irena was suggested by a story Jean-Claude told me about himself. Irena's husband, Edmund, a theatre critic, is obviously me, essentially a bystander. Carlotta is an imaginary member of the Open Theatre. The play-within-the-play by Art Maginnes (the Joe character) is entirely imaginary, although the idea of the 200-year-old man was Jean-Claude's. (I don't think he ever got around to writing it himself.) Saïd's final speech was directly inspired by Jean-Claude's monologue in the car one time as we were driving back to his mountain property from the village.

The idea of half life was also, I have to admit, a judgment on the single life from the self-congratulatory perspective of my marriage-with-children, which indeed was the way I wanted to live. Needless to say, not everybody needs to make the same choice, but I love love and have always felt that the closeness of the other is vital to my well-being and self-realization. Half life also suggests, of course, a very long time.

The play is conventional in form, imagined for a theatre with the resources to realize its multiple sets, which provide a large part of its theatricality. This is not the kind of physical theatre that Joe and Jean-Claude helped invent, which can be done on a bare stage. The play-within-the-play is in my own more verbal experimental style, influenced more by Brecht, Ionesco, and Beckett than Joe's ideas about acting.

Half Life was another breakthrough, more direct about emotion and intimacy than anything I had written before. I had more experience now to draw on. There is a comic poignancy to this play, a Stoic recognition of unsatisfied yearnings even in success as life keeps going right along.

I was wary of offending Jean-Claude, with whom I had a slightly prickly, competitive relationship, at least in my own mind, although in reality he was unfailingly generous to me. The play borrowed from his life as he told me about it and let out feelings I didn't want my friend to be confronted with, and for years I didn't show *Half Life* to anyone, fearing it might come to his attention. When I published it on my website decades later, and told him about it, he was not interested, though we remained close from afar.

The whole of *Half Life* has never been produced, but in 1994, a decade after it was written, when I had the chance to do a one-act at Ensemble Theatre Company in Santa Barbara, I extracted the inner, experimental play and presented it under the title *Come In Here*. By conicidence, Dick Spahn, the activities director from Riggs who had mentored my first directing almost forty years earlier, turned up living in Santa Barbara, and I had him play the main character, although he was twenty years too old for the part. It was too

sweet to resist closing the circle by directing him in a play. No telling what anybody made of it; even embedded in *Heavy Pockets*, this play-within-a-play is fragmented and allusive, with a far-fetched premise. It functions as an abstract, quasi-musical structure of light and dark, in contrast with the semi-realism of the rest of the play—an oddity, a discontinuity, a call-out for the joy of reckless modernism.

Translation
Agatha

A copy of Marguerite Duras's two-character play, in French, was given to me in 1983 by Pascale Cheminée, a lexicographer from Paris who came to work at the harpsichord shop for a time and became a part of Michele's and my family. The play is about a brother and sister looking back on the incestuous shared passion of their youth, which still possesses them. They meet in winter at their family's summer house on the Atlantic coast; she is leaving him, leaving France. Nothing happens; it is principally a monologue by the woman. I imagined there must be a back-story to Pascale's interest in this play beyond her admiration for Duras, but I never learned exactly what it was. In any event, I wanted to read it, because I liked Pascale, and again found that the best way to read in a language I don't know was to write it out in English. (I had three years of French in school, and some of it stuck.) I loved Duras's simple, exquisitely subtle language and the Brahms waltz that figures in the action; I was fascinated by the emotional stalemate the play depicts, unbearable intensity sustained, with no place to go. Pascale came for another visit the following year and we worked through my translation together; she was offended when I took liberties with Duras and scrupulously corrected my text.

I could not imagine this totally static play working in the theatre. It would be as unbearable for the audience as the characters' sorrow is for them. Duras did her own 1981 film of *Agatha* entirely in voice-over, against sublime images of the French seacoast in winter, with the actors drifting through the abandoned hotel they are remembering. (Duras herself voiced the woman.) I thought the only hope for it on stage would be to have actors of such charisma and magnetism that the audience would be happy just looking at them for an hour.

My unauthorized translation of *Agatha* was performed for a week at the Changing Scene in Denver in 1991. I was not there to see it and never got the whole story of what went down. I suspect it was a disaster.

One Hundred Thousand Songs

I had learned about Buddhism from a few friends who led the way. Diane di Prima did a Bardo reading from the *Tibetan Book of the Dead* after our friend Freddie Herko committed suicide in 1964. Jean-Claude's high school friend Tania Leontov went to Scotland to study with Chogyam Trungpa Rinpoche, a young Tibetan lama who had fled the Chinese invasion and studied at Oxford. She introduced me to meditation in a pub on Sloane Square in London, explaining the basic breath-counting technique. Diane moved to San Francisco in 1967 to study Zen with Suzuki Roshi. I followed a year later and lived in her house in the Haight for six months, sitting zazen at the

Zen Center every morning. Diane, Jean-Claude, and Diane's husband Alan Marlowe became students of Trungpa and took me along to his talks in Vermont and Colorado. The Buddhist view made perfect sense to me, and I internalized it as well as I could short of joining a Buddhist community. I have never been a joiner; I am sorry now that I have never been a member of a club. Raised a conventional country-club Christian—first Baptist, then Episcopalian—I sporadically attended Westerly Friends Meeting with Michele and our boys and described myself as a Sufi Buddhist.

Milarepa, a renowned 12th-century Tibetan yogi and poet, is seen as the ideal bodhisattva. His extraordinary life and character caught my interest for deep affinitive reasons that had little or nothing to do with my own person or immediate situation. I was inspired to write his life as an opera, imagining a musical score that would combine the eclectic minimalism of Brian Eno or Steve Reich with the clash, blare, and unearthly drone of traditional Tibetan horns, voices, and percussion. Aiming at spectacle, I treated myself to the resources of the Metropolitan Opera, imagining a vast thangka-like backdrop with buddhas in niches, a cast of dozens, choruses, festive processions, rainbows, flying, a collapsing house. The story of Milarepa's hard-won transition from furious youth to inspiring holy man is fascinating but proved to be extremely unwieldy, lacking any dramatic shape. My draft libretto was far too long and impossibly wordy. I was prepared to hack it into shape but never found a composer to work on it with, and nothing ever came of it. I loved writing it. Merely thinking about Milarepa brings enlightenment.

Directing
A Shot in the Dark, Curse of the Starving Class

In 1985 we lost our beautiful rented house in Westerly, Rhode Island, five miles from the harpsichord shop in Stonington, and Michele, who had been increasingly unhappy and restless, moved with Julian and Alfred to Las Vegas, New Mexico. I was still working for David Way, putting together actions for Mozart-era fortepianos. Without a family, for the first time in years I had time to do theatre. I eased my way back into it by directing a community-theatre production of *A Shot in the Dark*, a French farce adapted into a Broadway comedy (and a Peter Sellers movie). It was not my idea—I wanted to do Beckett or something of my own: they picked the play and hired me to direct it. The theatre was an old-fashioned community hall with a raised stage; I turned the space around, facing the audience the other way, using the architecture to suggest the courtroom setting. It was no fun driving to and from Kingston every weeknight for a month, but the rehearsals went smoothly, the actors doing whatever I suggested, and I think everyone had a good time. Doing it reminded me how much I love directing, how easily it comes to me, how I spring to life working with actors, how much I care about making it true and good, playing with space and forms and light, bringing an imaginary reality alive. I had sorely missed it.

Friends of mine organized a meteorite-viewing party in August 1985 on the Stonington breakwater. We went out in boats and climbed up onto the flat top of the square platform at the north end for our picnic. The fog came in before it was even dark so we couldn't see a thing, a joke on us, but we had a good time anyway. One of the guests was a theatre professor at Connecticut College. In the fog I boldly suggested to her that the college invite me to guest-direct a play, perhaps something by Sam Shepard. To my amazement, they took me up on it.

On the fifth of October I turned fifty and finally bowed out of my increasingly perfunctory job at the harpsichord works. So it was perfect timing. Initially I proposed to do *The Tooth of Crime*, a brilliant, challenging play that hadn't made much sense in Richard Schechner's environmental production at the Performing Garage in New York. The students rightly protested the small, virtually all-male cast so instead we did *Curse of the Starving Class*, a much better choice. The first of Sam's three relatively naturalistic "family plays," it is strongly felt, cunningly structured, studded with punchy images. I love Sam's plays, and this is one of his best.

Set in the kitchen of an old-fashioned farmhouse in the San Bernardino valley, where Sam grew up, *Curse of the Starving Class* is an intimate family drama. It was a challenge to envision it on the capacious stage of Conn College's Palmer Auditorium, which is better suited to dance. My solution was to open the stage up wide and isolate the kitchen, framed in a sharply defined wedge of bright light, against an enormous backdrop copied from a famous Ed Ruscha painting (without the words). With the huge sky behind it and a very low horizon line, you sensed that the lonely house stood on a rise, surrounded by empty space. The tech staff and students at the college did everything I asked, and it looked great.

Auditions revealed strong talent among the students, some of them already experienced and charismatic. The boy I cast as

Wesley, the son, was not an actor but a handsome young soccer player who had come to the audition on a dare. Sam kicked off the play with a deliberate shock to wake up the audience and alert them
that anything can happen when Wesley takes out his dick and pisses on his sister's 4-H project downstage center (we made him an "appliance").

I enjoy student acting. The inescapable drawback is that the parents are the same age as the children. Given that limitation, I thought I did a first-rate production of *Curse of the Starving Class*. It made me feel I was still myself.

Trouble

I moved back to New York in 1986, going to work as Assistant Press Secretary to Mayor Ed Koch. I was scarcely qualified for this job, having been out of the city for more than a decade and never having taken much interest in municipal politics. I needed a job, though, and when Dan Wolf, a close advisor to Koch, gave me an opening, I couldn't afford to say no. Besides, it sounded like an adventure, and I was ready for something new, my livelihood and beloved family having self-destructed, leaving me stranded in Rhode Island.

Julian had been living with me in Westerly. After an awkward transition as he finished fourth grade, he joined Alfred out west with Michele, and I moved in with my painter friend Gwen

Fabricant in Westbeth, the artists' live-work community in the West Village where I had always wanted to live. Joe Chaikin lived upstairs. I was happy to reconnect with the cosmopolitan intellectual vitality of New York, which I had missed in my decade-long exile.

My job in the Mayor's press office demanded that I be on hand at City Hall from nine to five, turned out in a suit and tie, plus I was on call via beeper one day most weekends. I had imagined I could use this job to transition back into the theatre, but I got caught up in it, locked in by the salary—$40,000 a year, the most I had ever made—and I stayed for the whole of Koch's final term. The job was fun at times, at times surreal, and brought with it a new identity: Gwen's lively circle of friends persisted in seeing me as a politico, not an artist like most of them. I had no time to do theatre, especially after Julian and Alfred came to live with us the following year.

I kept writing. I had a backlog of unproduced playscripts so it hardly made sense to write more plays. I collaborated on a new, New York iteration of *The Beggar's Opera* called *Bum Rap*, which seemed like a good idea, but it didn't go anywhere, and the moment passed. I revised my Tibetan opera, imagining Ondine as Milarepa's fearsome teacher Marpa. I launched into a long-form memoir of my amazing friends and lovers. I wrote one new play in this four-year period, *Trouble*, a series of scenes about the Bess Myerson scandal, but I had to keep it under wraps while I was working for the Mayor.

It came from direct experience. The afternoon of my first day in the Mayor of New York's Press Office, May 5, 1986, I was delegated to monitor an interview with Herb Ritman, the Assistant Mayor specializing in gay and cultural affairs, by Marsha Kramer, the City Hall reporter for the *Daily News*, a blonde bombshell (pardon the expression) with long scarlet fingernails, stiletto heels, and a terrible cold. Marsha was inquiring about a lunch Herb had had with Hortense Gabel, a respected liberal judge, whose oddball daughter, Sukhreet, had been hired as a personal assistant by Bess Myerson, the city's Commissioner of Cultural Affairs. Myerson, the first Jewish Miss America, had been a constant companion of Ed Koch—his "beard," as the saying goes—during his reelection campaign, countering suspicions that he was gay. Sukhreet's mother, ruling on the divorce settlement of Bess Myerson's boyfriend, Carl Capasso, sharply reduced his alimony.

I listened in on the conversation, tape-recording it so there could be no disputing what was said. Marsha was apologetic but probing. Herb was slippery and defensive. I had no idea what was going on but in the following months watched this rather sordid little drama blossom into the "Bess Mess," a scandal and embarrassment for the Mayor that led to Myerson's resignation and indictment by U. S. Attorney Rudy Giuliani. (She was acquitted.)

I was not, of course, allowed to write satirically about City Hall while I was working for the Mayor, but this was too juicy. *Trouble*, written under the alias Vernon O'Ray, is four vignettes rather than an actual drama. I later persuaded myself this would work as a form, letting the story, then well known, be glimpsed in fragments rather than laid out directly.

The first scene drew on an encounter I witnessed personally on the occasion of the gala reopening of Carnegie Hall. Ed rendezvoused with Bess in the lobby of a Chinese restaurant on West Fifty-Seventh Street, whence they traveled by horse-drawn carriage a block east to Carnegie Hall for a photo op, entering together up the flood-lit red carpet, parting in the lobby to go out to dinner with other people before the concert. It was obvious play-acting; they were mutually suspicious and barely speaking at this point. Little was said in my hearing, but I had no trouble making up a scene, light-heartedly putting myself into it as "Dickie," a gay Cultural Affairs sub-commissioner and sidekick to "Tess."

The drolly farcical second scene is a visit by the aging beauty queen to Andy Warhol's famous Factory. This is blatantly counter-historical—the heyday of Andy's factory was more than a decade earlier—but I didn't let that stop me. When I later did the play in New York, with Jimmy Camicia playing "Sandy Morphol" in the inescapable silver wig, this was everyone's favorite scene. The third scene is a monologue for Tess, set in her office in the former Huntington Hartford Museum with its distinctive porthole windows, part of the time talking on the telephone with her lover, "Randy," fighting for love and dignity as the situation collapses. She brings in a couple of staff members to review grants but doesn't allow them to say a word. The fourth scene takes us to a prison cell in Allentown, Pennsylvania, where Randy is doing time for tax fraud. As Tess clumsily tries to spring him by bribing a guard, she realizes her glamor has sadly expired. I was touched.

It would be ten years before I managed to put it on.

Lighting
I and I, The Tablets, Rules of Civility, Ancient Boys

In the fall of 1989 Johnny Dodd, suffering from AIDS and not strong enough to light the Living Theatre's new production, asked me to take his place as their lighting designer and do the lights for their next play.

I had a history with the Living Theatre going back to the early sixties, when Judith Malina and Julian Beck did a series of far-out, poetic plays at their theatre on Fourteenth Street. Jerry Tallmer, my mentor as a critic, considered them the most important theatre in New York. Their work, strongly influenced by German expressionism, made a tremendous impression on me. I covered the dramatic closing of the Living Theatre by the IRS in 1963, which drove the company into peripatetic exile in Europe for the next decade. I spent a month with them in 1966 in Berlin, Venice, and Amsterdam and wrote a book about the experience (*Theatre Trip*). I named my first son after Julian Beck. After his death in 1985, I came in from Westerly a few times to meet with Judith and Hanon Reznikov, her longtime lover and collaborator, in their apartment on West End Avenue to discuss what the Living Theatre should do next. I joined the board when they incorporated and witnessed Judith and Hanon's wedding.

In the new Living Theatre on East Third Street, Judith was directing *I and I*, an intense, ambitious, hallucinatory play written in 1945 in Jerusalem by Else Lasker-Schüler. By then I had transferred from the Mayor's press office into speech-writing, which left my weekends free. Alfred had gone back to Michele for sixth grade, Julian was starting high school and increasingly independent, and Gwen was teaching in Maine, so I had more time. Every day I hurried over to the theatre as soon as I finished at City Hall and hand-crafted the lighting for *I and I*, which took several weeks to come together. Judith loved to smoke pot and was sometimes highly discursive. But don't get me wrong: she was a great director, a great theatre artist. It was a privilege to know and work with her.

Set in a nightclub hell, *I and I* conflated Faust with the Nazis, an obvious idea once you think of it. Judith wanted the stage to "glitter darkly" so I taped up tiny red Christmas lights all over the black pipe-scaffolding set. I positioned strip lights on end at the sides and blasted the stage with hot color. I kept a soft follow-spot on the black Mefistofeles to make him visible next to the pale blond Faust. I personally moved and refocused every one of the lights at least once. The theatre was impossibly too small for this epic play, but the roughness of the production added an abrasive, confrontational quality that suited the material. No one I knew liked *I and I*; I thought it was extraordinary.

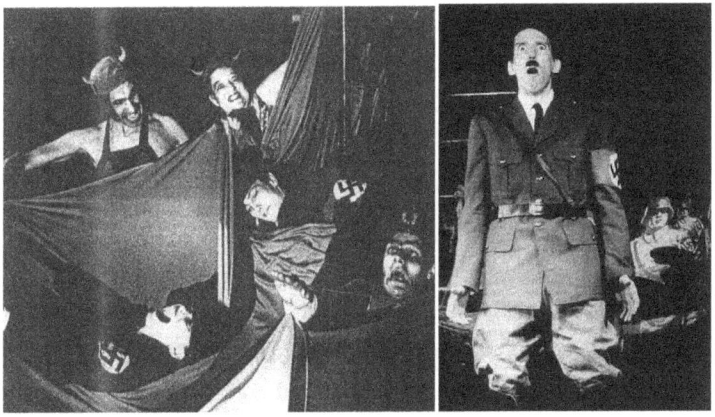

Johnny, constantly needing equipment to do lighting for his impecunious friends, had set up a stage light rental company he subsidized out of his marijuana business. (He donated a whole lighting setup to the new Living Theatre in honor of Julian Beck.) When Koch lost the primary later in the fall and my city job faded away, I slid over to running Johnny's lighting shop in a former meat locker in the meat-packing district, a ten-minute walk up Washington Street from Westbeth. Business was slow but steady, and it was sweet to be working for my long-ago lover and closest friend, though he was unwell and proved to be a moody, difficult boss.

It was a difficult year altogether. Gwen was in and out of the city, frustrated that she couldn't paint, Julian was cutting school and hanging out with druggies in Central Park, and I didn't really want to be in New York. This didn't feel like what I should be doing at the age of fifty-four.

When Judith and Hanon invited me to join the company and go on tour with them in Europe in the summer of 1990, I couldn't wait to go. And what an adventure it was! There were twenty-two of us, touring *I and I* and an earlier work of Hanon's, *The Tablets*, for which I strove to recreate Johnny's beautiful lighting. In New York the Living Theatre was disregarded, barely scraping along; in Europe we were honored artists, housed, fed, feted, and admired. We opened at a festival in Chieri, in Italy, and went on to Augsburg, Malaga, Berlin, Brno, and Prague. Every theatre was a new challenge for me, varying from a circus tent to a palace courtyard to an opera house. The day of setup would be incredibly hard work, and the performances were intense, and there was time in between to enjoy being in Europe, which I loved. Working was much better than being a tourist. Hanon had rented a van for the set, two vans for the actors, and I had the pleasure of riding in (often driving) the family car, with Judith, Hanon, and Isha Manna Beck, Judith and Julian's fiery 20-year-old daughter. I was a generation older than everyone except Judith and feeling my age, my left hip barely meeting its demands. I was not close to any of the company, but they were kind to me and appreciated my hard work. Judith and Hanon liked to squeeze in little side trips between gigs to look at art. They had lived in Europe for many years and knew how to enjoy it.

Back in New York, the Living Theatre's next show was *Rules of Civility*, Hanon's stylish, witty staging of a text by George Washington. I lit it in red, white, and blue, naturally, devising a geometrical pattern of downlights that synchronized with the stylized movement. As usual, the Living Theatre actors came off the stage and invaded the audience so the whole room got the red, white, and blue treatment too.

Johnny had fired me from the lighting company when I left on tour. The Living Theatre gave us a per diem in Europe but I wasn't paid in New York and had no money coming in. Jean-Claude providentially hired me to light his new play *Ancient Boys* in the La Mama Annex, which was a welcome challenge, although the play was not well directed. I did a highly detailed lighting design and have never known if it was good or not because I left immediately after the opening night performance, flying to Europe for a second tour with the Living Theatre, opening *Rules of Civility* in Rome two nights later.

Rules of Civility concluded with two George Washingtons (played by Isha and Tom Walker in period costumes and perukes) leading the company and audience out into the street to protest the Gulf War, which had begun just as we arrived in Rome. On opening night much of the audience joined the actors in marching down to the Via Veneto for a five-minute candlelight vigil across the street from the darkened, hulking American Embassy. The police arrived immediately with flashing blue lights, but we had made our point. The next day I went along with Hanon to a meeting with the police commissioner, who sat behind his desk playing with a large knife and said he would close us down if we did it again. After that our protest was confined to the quiet street in front of the theatre.

Hanon managed the relentless demands of touring with admirable ingenuity and grace. This was a far easier tour than the last one. *I and I* had a sprawling pipe-scaffolding set that took hours to set up; by contrast, *Rules of Civility* used a simple set of long curtains painted long ago by Julian Beck that could be hung up in minutes. We played a series of dates in Italy, some of them one-night stands, with whole weeks in Rome, Naples, and Sardinia, motoring through Austria for two stops in Hungary. I love Italy, especially the smaller Italian cities. Just being in Italy makes me happy. Regrettably, Judith was not with us this time, stuck in Hollywood acting in *The Addams Family* to support the Living Theatre in New York.

Life Before Death

When I had time I made one of my periodic visits to my parents in Santa Barbara. They had sold their house and moved into a life-care retirement community. They were comfortable there, all their needs nicely taken care of, but communication between them had sadly broken down. My ninety-year-old father was frail and barely mobile, having been injured in the surf in Acapulco when he was eighty; my dear mother, ten years younger, felt trapped and resentful and was drinking too much, barely coherent after the cocktail hour. Deep into middle age myself, I ought to have had some perspective, but dinners with them in their apartment challenged my equanimity. Sympathizing with both of them, I felt jerked around like a floppy doll and staggered out into the fragrant night air reeling.

I wrote about this painful phase of our lives as directly as I could. My previous plays about family were fiction; this was close to literal reality, for better or worse. *Life Before Death* was conceived as a play for television, dollying in real time between my parents' three rooms at the Casa Dorinda, written in a style I thought of as television realism. Regrettably, the days of live television drama were long gone, and the play has never been seen.

Lighting
The Zero Method

Gwen's brother died, my cat died, my car died, Johnny Dodd died, and soon after that my father died. My mother was alone on the West Coast. Alfred loved Santa Barbara and wanted to live with me for high school. I was broke, couldn't get along with Gwen, didn't want to grow old in New York City. So I decided to move west and start again.

Before leaving New York for good, in January 1992, I designed the lights for two more shows for the Living Theatre, first their 40th Anniversary Benefit at Cooper Union, then Hanon's exquisite play *The Zero Method* at the theatre on East Third Street. Hanon was a serious intellectual, deeply read in philosophy, history, and political theory. *The Zero Method* merged

Wittgensteinian ideas with the story of Hanon and Judith's romance in the Living Theatre, touchingly told in a quizzical, slippery noir style. The play moved through multiple locales across a wide, shallow stage, each of them wanting its own light. At one point Hanon's script demanded "light waves"; Judith suggested "peacock colors." Her sole personal request was that I make her look beautiful. I was inspired and stayed to run the  dimmer board myself for ten days, playing a trio with two of my heroes and favorite humans. Then I turned the dimmers over to Gary Brackett, loaded my battered possessions into a rented truck, and drove west.

Act IV

The Dinner Show

It wasn't long before I had a highly agreeable life going in Santa Barbara. I linked up with a new partner, Carol Storke, a person I could unreservedly love, respect, and actually get along with. Carol had a house in Goleta, and Alfred came and lived with us. I had a pleasant, theoretically half-time job as arts editor and music critic of *The Santa Barbara Independent*, a lively weekly newspaper with roots in *The Village Voice*.

There was a bustling theatre scene in Santa Barbara—two energetic college theatre departments, a small, good-quality professional theatre, a few independents coming and going, and many good actors. At the end of my first season at the *Independent* I started the annual "Indie" Awards, which brought the theatre community together for an award ceremony and party. I was friendly with the leaders of the various companies, but once again I was valued more as a media connection than an artist. None of them could be persuaded to let me direct in his theatre or would seriously consider putting on one of my plays. It was frustrating. I didn't want to just be a journalist, but I couldn't find my way in.

Finally, in 1996 an independent company called Dramatic Women invited me to contribute to an evening of ten-minute plays. Conveniently, I stumbled upon a short one-act called *The Dinner Show*, which I had written in a notebook at Charlemont in 1974, shortly before Michele and I got married.

The play, about a young couple hosting their first dinner party, is seriously whimsical and surreal, its light tone barely covering a sense of wildness beneath the surface, its Absurdism more Ionesco than Pinter or Beckett. The young bride turns into Pocahontas, and the dinner guests arrive carrying potted trees in front of their faces.

The producer, Bob Potter, a playwright and theatre professor at UCSB, suggested having one of his students, Maurice Lord, direct *The Dinner Show*. I went to see Maurie's student production of *Icarus's Mother* by Sam Shepard, which I had directed at the Caffè Cino in 1965, and thought his version truer than mine. Much as I enjoy directing, at that point I preferred not to direct my own plays: I had been forced to in the past because I couldn't find a director who grasped my intentions and would give me what I asked for. Maurie got it right away, and he cast and directed my little play perfectly.

Fast Forward

I wrote *Fast Forward* for *Santa Barbara Confidential*, Dramatic Women's 1999 program of ten-minute plays "about Santa Barbara." Too busy at home to think, I went to New York to write it, staying at a bargain hotel on Eleventh Street in the Village, seeing a few friends, and wandering around my old haunts.

The play is a first-person monologue recollecting my many loyal visits to Santa Barbara beginning in 1953, the year my family moved there and sent me east to Yale, until I moved there myself in 1992. My parents periodically appear in pantomime, my little sister Bicky represented by a doll. I wrote it straight off over several days with a ballpoint pen on four pages of a legal pad sitting cross-legged on my hotel room bed.

The tone is light, simple, dry, factual. It is amusing at first, then gradually and unexpectedly turns into a condensed, poignant representation of aging as the years roll by. My father is increasingly  frail and by the end has died. In the final image, my avatar brings my unspeaking mother on in a wheelchair, nibbling her favorite After Eight mints, and declares plainly, as was the fact, "Here I still am." Maurie directed a sensitive, exquisite rendition of this little playlet at Center Stage Theater, with Jay Carlander, a graduate student in history at UCSB, perfectly charming as me and Kinsey Packard and David M. Brainard representing my mother and father. I was entirely pleased.

Producing *Trouble, Buried Child, Criminal Genius* and *Featuring Loretta, Escape from Happiness*

I told Julian that the only thing missing in my new life was that I wasn't doing theatre. He said, "What's stopping you?" Nothing but inertia, I realized. If I was going to do the plays I wanted to do, including my own, I was going to have to produce them myself. Now the editor of *Santa Barbara Magazine*, I had joined the board of the stately Lobero Theatre, built in 1924, an icon of Santa Barbara's signature Spanish Colonial Revival architectural style. The theatre needed help raising $1 million plus for seismic reinforcement. Coached by the executive director, I taught myself the basics of producing by presenting a benefit recital by the eminent pianist Jerome Lowenthal, an old friend of my mother's. We made $30,000. I learned from this experience that the first step is to write a budget, which not only shows how much money you need but lays out all the many matters that need to be taken care of to make a show actually happen.

My first venture as an independent producer would be *Trouble*, directed by Maurie Lord. I really liked this little play—I thought it was funny and appalling and poignant, and I was tickled by its experimental form. Thus in April 1998, ten years after writing it, I produced *Trouble* at Center Stage Theater in Santa Barbara. Center Stage was a well-equipped black box theatre in the Paseo Nuevo, a downtown shopping mall, built and supported by the developers as a negotiated arts amenity. These would be the two theatres I repeatedly did plays at in Santa Barbara: the Lobero, 600 seats, traditional proscenium stage, upper-crust audience, highly visible; and Center Stage, 100 seats at most, flexible, classless, below the radar of the unadventurous.

At the Caffè Cino, La Mama, Theatre Genesis, and the Changing Scene, there had always been somebody behind me making sure the bills were paid and vouching for my sincerity. Producing on my own was a new experience—renting the theatre, hiring actors, designers, and crew, managing the publicity, making all the decisions, solving whatever problems came up, raising the money and paying the bills, taking full responsibility on myself. I put "Genesis West presents" on the program, but it was really just me.

Sets were a problem at Center Stage because there was no place to build or store scenery, and there was no one in the business of building scenery in Santa Barbara. *Trouble* is imagined for a bare stage with a small number of signifying set pieces, which the carpenter we hired overbuilt so they were difficult to hoist or move. The one set I really wanted was the ornate Chinese restaurant lobby for the opening scene, but nobody would buy into the idea and it didn't happen.

Maurie did a snappy job of directing *Trouble*, despite all kinds of headaches. The charismatic actress we hired to play Tess refused to say "fuck" in case her children were in the audience—Myerson was famous for swearing—and she never did properly memorize her monologue. We misguidedly double-cast a single actor as the Mayor ("Big Boy") in Scene 1 and Tess's lover Randy in Scene 4;. Refusing to wear a wig to decisively change his appearance, he seemed to be one character, confusing the already confused audience. I leveraged my editorship of *Santa Barbara Magazine* to persuade semi-famous Ben Bottoms to play Dickie. He proved a prima donna, insulting the costume designer, who wanted to take him to the thrift shop, insisting we buy him a suit at Saks. He went on opening night wearing two ties and mismatched shoes. He refused to present Dickie as gay, although Dickie was in fact based on a gay official at Cultural Affairs.

Despite all that, the play was amusing and the form worked, I thought, although the story was hard to follow and made little sense to non-New Yorkers.

Producing *Trouble* cost $9,500—$3,000 for the theatre, $3,000 for the actors, $2,500 for the set, plus other expenses—and took in a total of $4,900, including $1,000 from Carol and a few smaller contributions. I made up the difference. It was quite a change from the old days, when putting on show cost essentially nothing. I didn't like losing money, believing in principle that good theatre should pay for itself with ticket sales. Fortunately I could afford it.

Now that we had the germ of a theatre company, Maurie and I took to meeting for coffee once a week on the back terrace at our favorite downtown coffee house, the Caffè Siena. One day we were talking about my old friend Sam Shepard. Maurie had just read *Buried Child*, which had won Sam the 1979 Pulitzer Prize. More than anything in the world, he said, he wanted to direct a production of it. I responded with a rash spontaneity: "Why don't we do it at the Lobero?" It seemed a pity that plays were no longer being done there. The Lobero's big, well-equipped stage would be perfect for *Buried Child*.

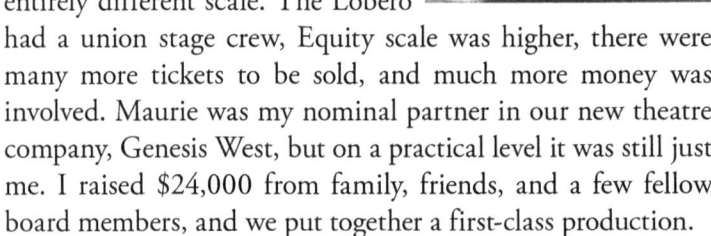

This would be producing on an entirely different scale. The Lobero had a union stage crew, Equity scale was higher, there were many more tickets to be sold, and much more money was involved. Maurie was my nominal partner in our new theatre company, Genesis West, but on a practical level it was still just me. I raised $24,000 from family, friends, and a few fellow board members, and we put together a first-class production.

Intimidated by the Lobero, I hired a professional designer to handle the set and lighting. He snowed me with his experience, then went missing at key moments doing other gigs. His design was fine, but everything was much harder than it might have been. I imagined he would take care of everything, then found myself driving a flatbed truck to North Hollywood to bring back a stack of used twelve-foot television flats. The Lobero stage crew had to figure out how to erect the extra-tall walls when his method didn't work. I wished I had done the lighting myself.

The set looked good, finally, and supported the play, and Maurie skillfully and boldly directed the exceptionally fine cast in a powerful rendition of Sam's complex, painfully emotional story. I was amazed by the quality of the actors available to us in Santa Barbara; there were extraordinary performances in all of our productions.

Buried Child was deservedly well reviewed and much admired. Even so, we didn't sell enough tickets to fill the seats or come close to covering the costs. I spent $39,000 on the production of *Buried Child*, made $14,000 at the box office, and thanks to the underwriters nearly broke even.

My friend David Gurin took me to see *The End of Civilization*, a play by George F. Walker, a Toronto playwright I had never heard of. It blew me away, not just the writing but the ferocious acting energy of the author's production at his home theatre, the Factory. This was one of a set of six plays, collectively titled *Suburban Motel*, Walker had set in the same motel room. Back home in Santa Barbara, I turned Maurie on to *Suburban Motel*, and we decided to do two of the plays for our next production, back at Center Stage Theater. I would direct *Featuring Loretta*, a comedy about a feckless young woman stranded in a cheap motel and two endearingly foolish fellows competing for her favor. Maurie would direct the rougher *Criminal Genius*, a farce about a bumbling gang and a tough woman cop. We could do them in repertory on the same set.

Genesis West was cultivating a core group of talented actors in sync with our aims, and we had gained enough cachet to put up first-rate casts. Kinsey Packard in the title role of *Featuring Loretta* was deliberately adorable in her red cowboy boots and endearingly vulnerable. Jay Carlander and Ted Harmand were delightful as her sleazy suitors and ClaireMarie Mallory wryly hilarious as the Russian maid whose father owns the motel. For *Criminal Genius*, Maurie had Leslie Gangl Howe, a witty, powerful favorite, and daring, persuasive Fred Lehto, as well as David Brainard and a couple of newcomers. It was a manageable production, and it clicked with audiences and reviewers. My balance sheet came out even.

The two comedies at Center Stage had been so much fun that we decided to follow up with a bigger play of Walker's, *Escape from Happiness*, in a bigger theatre, the Lobero.

I produced and Maurie directed. He put together a great cast and staged it brilliantly. He had become a very good director.

It was perpetually a problem for us to find rehearsal space and a place to build sets. In the case of *Escape from Happiness*, the solutions came in one package. An interesting designer named Kent Hodgetts agreed to design the set. He and his wife were restoring the beautiful Bernhard Hoffmann mansion above Mission Creek Canyon, designed by James Osborne Craig in 1921. Kent had claimed the garages as his studio and we could build the set there; Maurie would rehearse in the big music room at the unrestored end of the house. Kent designed an ingenious set of wall units connecting at different angles that stretched clear across the Lobero stage. He was very smart about figuring out the technology, and he and I built it together. We set it up in the driveway to make sure it worked, intending to take the pieces back inside to paint them.

Meanwhile Maurie was having a fine time rehearsing up at the house, with a high-powered cast of ten. Kent's wife was concerned about the beautiful end-grain floor of the music room so we put down heavy paper to protect it. Rehearsals inevitably get rambunctious as the actors throw themselves into the spirit of the action, and she grew increasingly up-tight about our invading her house. Abruptly, less than a week before we were due to move into the Lobero, they withdrew their hospitality. Kent told me to take the set away. Maurie quickly found an alternate space for the last few rehearsals, but if it rained, the set would be ruined. I rented a truck, and Alfred helped me disassemble it and truck it down to the Lobero, which found room to store it until we could move it onto the stage. Kent had disappeared leaving the walls unpainted. At the last minute I found a color sketch he had wordlessly left for us, which Maurie and I took to the paint store, matching the colors as best we could. The Lobero crew painted the set once it was up. The pink walls and turquoise trim were probably gaudier than Kent intended. I lit it myself and thought it looked great.

Escape from Happiness was a terrific production. The cast was spectacular. I loved the play, although it was probably half an hour too long, and I couldn't persuade Maurie to cut it. I was only sorry so few people saw it. Over six performances, the box office issued 463 tickets, 126 of them comps. Having tried it twice, we concluded after *Escape from Happiness* that the Lobero was too big for the kind of work we wanted to do and much too expensive for my means.

Dogs Bark All Night

The core of our audience in Santa Barbara was our fellow theatre artists, whom I generally had to comp—as I expected them to comp me—which made a considerable dent in the box office. As much as a third of the audience got in free, and at either theatre we had to pay a box office fee for each of their tickets. Producing was demanding, a couple of months of obsessive struggle, and every production cost me thousands of dollars. With Maurie directing other writers' plays, it was hard to think why I was working so hard and paying so much so other people could have the fun of doing the art. It was time to do another play of my own.

I was busy, editing *Santa Barbara Magazine*, reviewing concerts for the *News-Press*, vice president of the board of the Lobero as well as producing plays— not to mention visiting my aged and fading mother, riding my horse, and enjoying a full, happy home life. Feeling I had to get away from everything if I wanted to get any writing done, I went to Taos for two weeks in July 2000 and wrote *Dogs Bark All Night*. Julian, busy with his own life there, helped me find a room to rent in Talpa, a nearby adobe village (where a dog did bark in the night, giving me my title).

I was reading about war, thinking about war, haunted by images of burning oil wells in Kuwait and Iraq and the Highway of Death. I projected these feelings onto Janice, a made-up character who, like a few real women involved in violent protest in the late 1960s, went underground in the 1970s, creating a new identity, marrying, having a child, making a normal life. Now, horrified by photos of the Gulf War, she can no longer stay silent, speaks out, is arrested and imprisoned. Her husband and teenage son had no idea of her earlier identity.

The play juxtaposes Janice's burning political conscience with the quotidian comforts and stresses of the family: her son and husband at odds over soccer, her sister pregnant and coming out as a Lesbian. It was my most openly political play, and I wrote with a new directness about family matters as well. It required a wild and unwarranted leap of optimism to spin this story in a positive direction at the end: sweetly, the father has accepted the son as he is (gay), and Janice is running for president on an Idealist platform. In the final image, she addresses a campaign rally, backed by her proud family, before a big projection of a sunlit American flag waving in the breeze. Maurie directed and I lit a crisp production with heartfelt performances by some of our favorite actors—Laurel Lyle as Janice, David Brainard as Bill, Steven Gonzales as Tommy, and ClaireMarie Mallory as Bill's sister Vera.

Dogs Bark All Night turned out to be bizarrely timely: the entire run of performances took place after the 2000 election, when Al Gore won a plurality of the popular vote, and before the Supreme Court's decision six weeks later to award the presidency to George W. Bush, when it was still possible to be optimistic.

Producing/Directing
Mud and *The Danube, Krapp's Last Tape*

I introduced Santa Barbara audiences to one of my favorite contemporary playwrights, Irene Fornés, by presenting two of her fine plays at Center Stage Theater. Maurie would direct *Mud*, and I would direct *The Danube*. We devised a unit stage handily convertible to the two plays' different demands. Maurie's *Mud* was brilliant, winning him an Indie award for directing. My production of *The Danube* was the best work I have done.

Set in Budapest in the late 1930s, *The Danube* presents charming characters and a conventional love story, between an American student and the young Hungarian woman teaching him her language. As the play goes on, it is slowly taken over by some unnamed horror, the suave civility gradually invaded by nightmare, the characters incrementally ill, scruffy, goggled, crazed. The general critical interpretation has been that these are the after-effects of nuclear conflict; my own sense is that *The Danube* evokes the overwhelming of civilized life by the Nazi aggression and the Second World War, although this is never explicit. The play keeps its distance and remains inscrutable, suggesting far more than it declares, which can be frustrating for audiences not equipped with Keats's "negative

capability." (Frank Rich's denunciation in the *New York Times* is available on the web.)

I relished the non-naturalistic style of *The Danube* and took a scrupulously aesthetic approach to its demands. For the varied settings, I commissioned a superior artist to make a suite of woodcuts to be rear-projected onto the backdrop. Months in advance, I recorded a Hungarian actress pronouncing the language tapes Irene uses as the basis of her dialogue. I commissioned a young Polish cellist to compose and perform musical bridges between the scenes (with me on harpsichord). I had puppets resembling the actors made for the puppet scene. I hired a  first-rate costume designer, Mary Gibson. My son Alfred was stage crew, drilled to the inch in resetting the furniture between scenes, when wisps of smoke come up through the floor. I scrupulously realized all of Irene's specifications, and my actors responded with brilliantly stylistic performances, especially George Backman, a first-rate London-trained classical actor; Ken Gilbert, a bold physical actor; and Erica Kylander-Clark, a sensitive naturalistic actor. The fourth, Drew Murphy, lost his nerve and became uncontrollably self-conscious and self-critical. I tried everything to reassure him with no success. He was fine in the part but hard to keep afloat.

I loved *The Danube*, which has a depth of historical consciousness and sympathy that transcends the logic of words, doing the magic only theatre can do.

I had a second opportunity to direct *Krapp's Last Tape* when D. J. Paladino, a colleague at the *Santa Barbara Independent*, asked Robert Lesser, a fine actor, to perform it for his (D.J.'s) fiftieth birthday, which he was celebrating with a party at Center Stage Theater. They invited me to direct. I love this play with all my heart. Bobby and I dove into it with gusto, reading biographies of Beckett that made us admire and like him all the more. We staged the play with exquisite care. Much of it consists of Krapp revisiting excerpts from tape recordings he has made on previous birthdays. I ran the sound from a remote tape deck in the wings, synchronizing my cues with Bobby's operation of the dummy recorder on stage. His Krapp was  drier and more stylized than Bill Bolender's in Taos twenty-four years earlier and perfectly to my taste, sophisticated, humorous, and exquisitely poignant. I lit it starkly with two big spotlights on stands. We gave several more performances as part of the 2002 Lit Moon International Theatre Festival.

Lighting
Kiss of the Spider Woman, Happiness

How we hooked up I don't know, but I was always looking for interesting people. The guy, charismatic, with a New York edge, was an acting teacher with a secret method. He had a studio in Goleta and two young actors in his spell, and he was directing them in *Kiss of the Spider Woman*, the play version of Manuel Puig's wonderful novel. They had been working on it for months, their developing interpretation intense and excruciatingly slow. I loved the play and, hoping for the best, signed on to design the lighting for it at Center Stage Theater.

Center Stage's high grid facilitates the steep angle and long throw lighting designers normally like. *Kiss of the Spider Woman*, set in a prison cell, calls for something else. Brad Spaulding, the theatre's crack tech director, hung vertical pipes down from the grid at the corners of the stage for me to bring the lights in close, maximizing the intensity of these strangely entranced performances. I illuminated the sex scene at the lowest possible reading, the lights barely glowing, at the threshhold of visibility. There was nothing to say except it was what it was, the lighting possibly the best thing about it.

Maurie Lord had drifted away from our partnership in Genesis West. Hoping to persuade him to direct *Heavy Pockets*, I pulled together a reading in the Lobero rehearsal studio (a "romp," one of the actors called it); but the play didn't really work without real acting, and Maurie didn't really get it. We kept meeting for coffee every week but couldn't think of another play we wanted to do. In any event, I no longer had extra income to lose on producing plays. *Santa Barbara Magazine* had been sold, and I had resigned as editor. I was writing music reviews for the *Santa Barbara News-Press*, not looking for another day job.

Maurie landed a gig directing another George F. Walker play, *Happiness*, at Sacred Fools, an adventurous small theatre in Hollywood, and asked me to come down and light it. I love going into an unknown theatre and figuring out how to make a show work in it. Lighting *Happiness* was fun.

Turnip Family Secrets

Written in 1982 in my attic study in Westerly, Rhode Island, when my children were young, *Turnip Family Secrets* is a feel-good musical fantasy about a family of two parents and one child who move into an enormous turnip—inspired by the giant vegetables being grown at Findhorn in northern Scotland. I always insisted *Turnip Family Secrets* was a "play with music," not a musical, although there are in fact eighteen songs.

I imagined a complicated scenic scheme, like an animated children's book, with radical shifts of scale. A child actor could play the Giant and look big in relation to a tiny turnip; the same child could play the Turnip Fairy as a miniature leprechaun. The moment the play was finished, I wanted to see it produced, but at that point in my life I was completely out of the loop as a playwright, three hours from New York, locked into a full-time job. I attempted to set the songs to music myself. With a fellow shop-worker I toyed with the idea of starting a theatre in Mystic to put it on. I built a model and tried to figure out how to present it in the living room without success. So the play languished.

Twenty years later, in Santa Barbara, I was finally in a position to put it on. To my great delight Joe Woodard, a newspaper colleague and guitarist-songwriter of notable energy and originality, agreed to write music for the songs and what's more brought along his band of first-rate musicians, Headless Household, to play it.

Supporting a family, bringing up children, and keeping a marriage together is a challenge I was struggling with when I wrote this play. *Turnip Family Secrets* is escapism with an edge.

Seen through a child's eyes, Bess and Cal, the grown-ups, are romantic, sexy, idealized. Young David has the idea of hollowing out the turnip and moving in, and they do it, gleefully. Awake in the night, the boy wanders off by himself and comes back to find his turnip-house and parents have been snatched away by a hungry Giant. He is rescued by the Turnip Fairy, who teaches him to fly. The parents adapt to living in the uprooted turnip, lying on its side on the Giant's kitchen counter. Time moves much more slowly for giants. Human years later, David, now a sophisticated, gay New Yorker, comes home for a visit just as the Giant decides it is finally time to eat his tasty prey. At the last instant the Fairy intervenes again, magically transporting the little family to Venice, where we last see them peacefully drifting in

a gondola after a very good lunch.

This curious story springs from my tender fondness for the idea of family, for parents trying to do the right thing and have a good time, for the child trying to love them and be true to himself. Domestic tranquility is fragile: there are larger, dangerous forces and tendencies at play in the world, but also untold opportunities for bliss. My unwarranted confidence that grace and good fortune will save us when all seems lost reflects an inherited optimism I have never been willing to relinquish.

Producing *Turnip Family Secrets* would keep me too busy to direct as well. Maurie insisted he didn't know how to direct a musical (he may have been right, but I suspected he just didn't like it). I enlisted the director of a local children's theatre, who staged it skillfully. The set only partly realized my original vision, but what we managed to make was lovely. A giant turnip rose up out of the floor until it filled the stage. In the next scene, a tiny turnip glowed in a puddle of moonlight, dwarfed by the child-Giant looming over it. The lovers' bed was steeply canted toward the audience, as if seen from above, and bathed in moonlight. The Giant's nose sniffed out and terrified the innocent family. I designed the lights, and Brad made my visions come true. My son Julian, who as a child had written lyrics for the Giant's song for me, came from Taos and constructed a ten-foot knife that descended on the turnip living room to startling effect. Headless Household rendered

Joe's imaginative music on a scaffold raised above the back of the set, as in the Berliner Ensemble's *Threepenny Opera*. The songs were terrific, and the four members of the cast sang them beautifully, with gusto and tender feeling, embodying the characters with serious wit and vitality. It was a wonderful show.

Turnip Family Secrets would be the last of my Genesis West productions. I was finished with Santa Barbara, having written for all the publications in town and done enough theatre there. My sweetheart wanted to move to a place where she could have a barn for her horses. Our parents were gone, my children grown up, and I was ready to move on.

Act V

Translation
Victor, or Power to the Children

In April 2003 Carol and I moved to Silverton, Oregon, a quiet town in the Willamette Valley, well away from the interstate, settling on a small farm along Silver Creek on the edge of town. We remodeled and expanded the house, Carol built herself a horse barn and covered arena, and I converted the chicken house into a spacious writing studio. While all this work was being done, we lived in a rented house a mile away, and I had time on my hands, knowing no one in my new home town.

I had long before heard about the French play *Victor* from Paul Sand, who must have imagined himself playing the nine-year-old title character. It was probably 1962, the year the play was revived in Paris by Jean Anouilh. I eventually acquired a copy, in French and finally had time to struggle through it. Once more, as a way of reading a difficult text, I wrote out an English translation.

Roger Vitrac, the author, knew everyone in Paris in the twenties, joined the surrealist movement, and in 1926 teamed up with Antonin Artaud to found the Théâtre Alfred-Jarry, where they did many important contemporary experimental plays including *Victor*, "setting the tone for the Theatre of the Absurd, twenty years before Ionesco," according to Wikipedia.

Victor is a three-act domestic drama in the guise of boulevard comedy. Victor and his six-year old friend Esther have observed his father and her mother making love, and Victor, bratty, smart, and proud of being nine, uses this knowledge ruthlessly without really understanding anything. Esther's father goes mad. The play is both farce and tragedy, and I was tickled and touched by it, as well as admiring its straight-faced outrageousness. I longed to see it on the stage, but regrettably this kind of civilized entertainment is a thing of the past in America. There are several European renditions on the internet. My translation is crude, which may be a good thing in the case of this peculiarly charming play.

Directing
Beyond Therapy, A Midsummer Night's Dream (Abbreviated), The Flight of the Butter Boy, Trouble

Not far from our new home, on the road to Salem, I noticed the Brush Creek Playhouse, once a one-room schoolhouse, later a grange hall, now a community theatre. Thinking I might be able to put on plays there, I got in touch and was invited to a board meeting. They were about to open a production of *Come Back to the Five and Dime, Jimmy Dean, Jimmy Dean* and needed someone to do the lights. Naturally I volunteered. All they had was clip-ons and a few rotary household dimmers, but I made it look as good as I could and watched the entire run of this quirky comedy from the elevated light booth in the back of the theatre. The play was so badly miscast that you couldn't follow the plot. They justified this by calling it a "staged reading," although it looked like a production to me, albeit grotesquely inept.

I tried to think what I could do at Brush Creek Playhouse that would work on its tiny proscenium stage. I fancied I would introduce myself by directing *Beyond Therapy*, a frivolous comedy by Christopher Durang, and they gave me a date. I had a lot of fun with it. I knew what I was doing and didn't stress about it too much. There was considerable comic talent in the cast, and they mostly went along with my ideas (although the scatter-brained lead actress never did properly learn her lines). The show was light and funny and made a good impression on everybody who saw it. And it cost me nothing!

That led to an invitation to direct *A Midsummer Night's Dream* the following summer as a benefit for the Silverton Arts Association. I had always wanted to direct Shakespeare and leapt at the opportunity, on the proviso that someone else act as producer. The setting, at a wedding garden up in the hills, was appropriately sylvan, with chairs for the audience set out on a lawn, a pond to one side, a steep wooded hillside rising behind the platform stage. I abbreviated the play to just over an hour, cutting the mechanicals apart from Bottom, not knowing how to play them without condescension, and focused on love—the charming, confused romances among the four youngsters in the forest and the bitter love-battles of Theseus/Oberon and Hippolyta/Titania. I was blessed with intelligent, attractive actors for the mature roles and talented, likable high-schoolers for the youngsters. I had my heart set on a boy for Puck but wound up with a terrific young girl, who by acting a boy was more boyish than a real boy would have been.

I had of course seen countless Shakespeare productions through the years, many of them brilliant—Tyrone Guthrie's

Troilus and Cressida comes to mind, and Siobhan McKenna's *Hamlet*, and Richard Burton's, and the Mabou Mines *King Lear*, with Ruth Maleczech as Lear—I could go on. We had checked out the hugely popular Oregon Shakespeare Festival in Ashland, but I was put off by their tendency to overproduce and overact the plays, relentlessly illustrating the text with gestures and schtick. Shakespeare doesn't need that; the language does the work if you let it. Accordingly, we spent the first week of rehearsals sitting around a table under the walnut tree in our backyard making sure everyone knew exactly what they were saying and why before we started staging the play. Speaking the text clearly was more than half the battle.

A young choreographer made dances for the fairies. A team of hard-working wives and mothers made costumes. A local composer contributed incidental music. The drama teacher at the high school appeared one day to decorate the stage. The actors came through with lively, personable interpretations of the characters. The weather smiled on our two performances, and everything worked out. Shakespeare our contemporary was alive in the Oregon woods.

While I was still living in Santa Barbara, a young man working in the box office at the Lobero Theatre, Guy J. Jackson, gave me the script of a play he had written. *The Flight of the Butter Boy* was an odd, elaborate fable, much of it couched in a goofy invented language. I liked it very much and tried to interest Maurie in directing it, but with no success, and it would have been a costly undertaking in Santa Barbara, with a large cast and an elaborate set. Years passed before I found myself in a position to do it at the Brush Creek Playhouse.

Alfred, who had been studying acting at Santa Barbara City College, came up to play the romantic hero, Tobyus, and helped me build the scenery. I wanted to demonstrate an alternative to the boring box sets typical at Brush Creek. *The Flight of the Butter Boy* is set in an enchanted forest, and I devised a layout of overlapping trees and shrubbery with numerous entrance points. Alfred helped me set up the flats in a staggered, asymmetrical layout, and I asked a well-known local painter for help making it look like a forest. He drew profiles for narrow strips of plywood to add to the straight edges of the flats to give the shape of tree trunks; we cut them out and nailed them on. He sent us to the hardware store to buy four colors of paint, had us paint everything dark green, and the next day, in a few hours of daubing, transformed the stage into a dazzling impression of a forest. It turned out he had professional experience creating dioramas for the National Park Service. I lit the action at low angles from the side, greenishly, with very little front light. It looked amazing.

Casting gave me the greatest difficulty, which in the long run proved to be the fatal limitation of Brush Creek Playhouse. Actors had to be wooed and coaxed and the imagination greatly stretched to fit them into the roles. With enormous struggle I found good people and droll personalities to impersonate most of the characters in the play, but it proved excruciatingly hard to find anyone at all to impersonate the villain's girlfriend, an important role—it nearly scuttled the production. I wound up with a sullen, clueless, ultimately willing teenager who had never been on a stage before. She had a terrible time learning to speak the lines audibly and intelligibly without looking out into the audience for approval. In the long run I admired her  grit and grew fond of her rather excruciating performance. A handsome eleven-year-old boy was perfect for the title role. His mother, another neophyte, was also in the cast, and needlessly insecure: she was a natural. Without my asking she dyed the boy's hair yellow, a nice demonstration of commitment.

I was charmed by this production, delighted with the results of my efforts. *The Flight of the Butter Boy* is an original, amusing, inspired piece of writing, and we did a bang-up job with it. Audiences didn't know what to expect or what they had seen, but they couldn't help liking it.

Producing
Trouble

"Next time, New York," I said to Alfred at the end of the run of *Butter Boy*. Our work was getting good, and I wanted to show it to a more sophisticated audience. This spontaneous impulse led to our doing a production of *Trouble*, my play about the Bess Myerson scandal, at Theater for the New City in the East Village in the winter of 2006-07. Maurie had done his best with *Trouble* in Santa Barbara, despite some difficult actors, but it was a New York story; if it was going to make sense anywhere, it would be there.

Crystal Field at TNC, a mutually supportive friend since the early sixties, said I was welcome there. I calculated that the production would cost around $15,000 including two months of city living for Alfred and me. Wondering how to pay for it, it occurred to me that I had a Diane Arbus print that was worth some money, possibly even that much—a contact print of the topless waitress at the nudist camp, with a note on the back, that Diane had sent me at *The Village Voice* before her work was shown at the Museum of Modern Art in 1967. The picture had been sitting around in a frame for years, and I liked having it, but this seemed a creative use for it, and I sold it at Sotheby's for $13,000. Doing *Trouble* at TNC cost more than that, but I had such a good time with Alfred that I didn't mind the cost: it was worth it. Donald L. Brooks offered us his extra apartment at 43rd Street and Eighth Avenue, a block from Times Square, which was pleasant and affordable. An extravagantly bold designer, director, and producer from the late sixties onward, Donald was one of the singular talents who flourished in the

heyday of Off-Off-Broadway with almost no recognition.

This production of *Trouble* had its moments, but it was doomed from the start. To do justice to Bess Myerson's charisma, I needed a star, and regrettably I had nothing to offer a star. Having been absent from New York theatre for three decades, I had no useful contacts anymore, no base or bankable identity, no ongoing access to actors or production personnel, no support system at all. I had not realized what a handicap this would be. I went to New York for a week in October to watch the Sotheby's auction and cast the play. Crystal recommended an actress she knew to play Tess Byerson; she auditioned, and I thought she would be fine. Alfred would play Dickie, a rather swish, gushy character he could have fun with. I drafted Jimmy Camicia to play Sandy Morphol. Auditions for the other parts brought excellent actors.

Tech was a different story. Donald Brooks agreed to design the sets, but what I needed was someone to build it, and Donald couldn't do that. Mark Marcante of TNC kindly built me a skeletal revolving door, crucial for entrances, but I failed again to get the kitschy-elegant Chinese restaurant vestibule I wanted for the opening scene. Donald painted a show curtain to lower between scenes, unfortunately much too heavy and hard to hoist. I scrounged up props and costumes from the cellar storerooms. I desperately needed help but couldn't seem to get any. I tried to hire a stage manager without success; eventually one of the actors had to do it. I should have hired someone good to build me a set, likewise to do publicity, but I was trying to do it on the cheap. Jerry Tallmer interviewed me for *The Villager*, but that was all the press we got. I could have done the lighting myself if I'd had a competent electrician to work with, but I didn't know the setup, and I was seventy years old, and

the house guy wanted to do it himself. It looked and ran O.K., but he was a royal pain, half-drunk, slow, dithering, making me and the cast wait four hours to begin the tech rehearsal, which was inexcusable.

Trouble didn't make any kind of splash and played to embarrassingly small audiences. I had booked us for four weekends when two would have been plenty. The performances got very good at times, and I enjoyed watching them. But somehow nobody who saw the play quite got the point, including political friends, who were offended by its quizzical point of view toward civic life and the woes of fame. I was never able to take politics seriously, despite recognizing that it sometimes has serious repercussions.

My Tess proved to be emotionally fragile, still in mourning, it turned out, for her late husband. She did a professional job with the role, often bringing it considerable snap, but was frustratingly unavailable to me in rehearsal, disappearing in breaks to smoke alone in some dark corner, and too distracted to get on top of her lines in a timely way. I only slowly came to realize she had a drinking problem. One Saturday night two weeks into the run, the night my entire family had come from far and wide to see my play, Tess arrived twenty minutes past starting time drunk and blubbering. Apologizing to the audience for the delay, I helped get her dressed and talked her into going on, but the performance was chaos, Alfred and the other actors heroically coaxing her through her dialogue. I suffered through the first act and sat out the second in the lobby. That was also the night the critic from *Backstage* saw my play; he trashed it and me without apparently noticing the impaired condition of the star. What a fiasco!

The sad fact is, the moment had passed. Nobody cared about Ed Koch and the Bess Mess anymore. My bemused attitude made little sense to anyone but me. Audiences continued to trickle in, and most of the performances were quite sparkling. I was just doing it for fun, after all, having a fling in New York with my son. I did not mind too much that the play was a flop, only regretting that I still had not given *Trouble* the production that would do it justice.

Lighting
Blue Heart, Far Away, The Goat, The God of Hell

Genesis West went dormant for a few years after I moved away from Santa Barbara. Speaking from long experience, I had advised Maurie that if he wanted to direct the plays he liked, he was going to have to produce them himself. Eventually he realized I was right and revived the company with a series of productions at Center Stage Theater beginning in 2005. He brought me down from Oregon to do the lights for the first four of them. I loved working with Maurie and especially at Center Stage Theater, which had Brad Spaulding to hang and focus the lights and program and run the dimmer board. Brad and I had an excellent working rapport. He gave me everything I asked for.

Blue Heart by Caryl Churchill (the English Irene Fornés) was the challenging play Maurie selected to reinaugurate Genesis West. It consists of two one-act plays, *Heart's Desire* and *Blue Kettle*, the first about the disintegration of time, the second about the disintegration of language. This is an edgy, brainy breed of comedy, and Maurie gave the plays a stunning production, with brilliant acting by the Genesis West regulars, witty costumes by Mary Gibson, and a flashy revolving stage set by a smart designer, Tal Sanders. I won an Indie award for my colorful lighting design. Brad said there were more light cues than he'd had for any other show.

The next Genesis West show, *Far Away*, also by Caryl Churchill, presented a frightening world in which horrible things are happening just off stage, the grown-ups pretending evil is good. The play is creepy and *1984*-ish and also peculiarly fanciful. Much of the action is set in a hat factory where two artisans make fantastic hats—later to be worn by a parade of emaciated prisoners crossing the stage in a sinister parade, the hats subsequently to be "burned with the bodies." This called for expressive lighting of a starker character, which with Brad's help I was happy to supply.

When I saw Edward Albee's play *The Goat, or Who Is Sylvia?* in Portland, I didn't like it, but Maurie's production, with Robert Lesser as Martin and Leslie-Gangl Howe as his wife, Stevie, proved how great it really is. Albee's style is more realistic than Churchill's. Maurie made my life difficult by blocking the actors all the way over to the edges of the room. It is tricky to light the actors more than the scenery, and directors usually keep them away from the walls. I had to put up extra lights skimming the walls so the actors didn't disappear into shadow. It is the first obligation of lighting design to create an even zone of light for the actors to act in. Too often I've seen a dim spot right in the middle of the stage. Part of acting is finding the light.

The last of this sequence of projects with Genesis West was a new Sam Shepard play, *The God of Hell*, a ferocious exercise in political paranoia. I remember it as a simple lighting job, but it won me the following flattering notice from Charles Donelan, the theatre critic of the *Santa Barbara Independent*: "No review of *The God of Hell* would be complete without mentioning Michael Smith's incredible lighting. Smith has worked some real magic here, and everyone interested in innovative stagecraft will want to see it." Thank you, Charles!

Bad Dog

Janice, my revolutionary heroine, had been left up in the air at the end of *Dogs Bark All Night*, improbably running for president. I always knew that play needed a second act. What would happen now? So I wrote *Bad Dog*—another dog play without a dog, the title half-echoing *Dogs Bark All Night*, half-referring to our then president, W.

Janice has been in prison for seven years, prosecuted after all for her protests in the 1970s. She runs for president again, and thanks to a magical general awakening, she wins in a landslide. Her platform is everything I could think of that would be better than existing policies with their tragically warped priorities. *Bad Dog* is structured like *Trouble*, in four loosely linked, discontinuous scenes, but even floatier. I took myself to sparsely settled southeast Oregon to write it, trying to follow through on the idealistic dream.

I decided to do *Bad Dog* in Santa Barbara instead of making Alfred come to Oregon to act in it. It was wonderful to be back at Center Stage Theater, and I was fortunate to have the original actors, Laurel Lyle and David Brainard, as Janice and her supportive husband Bill. Alfred played Tommy, who has grown up, moved to New York, and is having a hard time. Susan Keller stepped in as his Aunt Vera, whose lover is being deported.

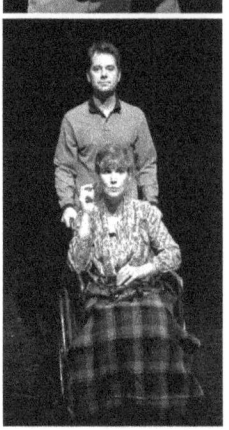

Bad Dog was short. To give people their money's worth, I added three earlier, unrelated short plays, which were performed between the four scenes, like this:

> *Bad Dog 1*
> *More! More! I Want More!*
> *Bad Dog 2*
> *Point Blank*
> *Bad Dog 3*
> *Fast Forward*
> *Bad Dog 4*

I called it *Bad Dog and Other Plays* and directed it myself.

More! More! I Want More! and *Fast Forward* are discussed above. *Point Blank*, which I wrote in a notebook around 1975, is an experimental "loop" play for eight actors, consisting of four minutes or so of dialogue and action meant to be repeated several times. The play was a conscious attempt to write about nothing, using the run-up to a typical

family picnic as the template. Until now I had never had an opportunity to put it on, and I wanted to see if it would work. I used the whole stage for it, lit it brightly against a bright green cyc, and blocked it geometrically: all movements were straight up and down stage, straight across, or on strict diagonals except for Grandma, tipsy on martinis, who moved in curves. Blank as the characters were, vivid personalities emerged from the presence of the actors in Mary Gibson's amusing costumes. It was funny and oddly poignant, a random snippet of busy life.

Whether *Bad Dog* itself was intelligible in this broken-up rendition I never really knew. The form of the evening was wildly experimental, pushing the limits of coherence—like watching a play on television and flipping away to something else during the commercials. It didn't seem to bother anyone. I thought it made *Bad Dog* stronger to break it up. I meant it as a strong statement about what should be, not just what is. I lit each of the segments in a different style and won another Indie for my lighting.

Summer Lightning

People in Silverton kept asking me when I was going to do another play. But it was heavy lifting to get anything on. I tried to fit in with the Brush Creek Players, paid my dues, but found little sympathy for my ideas and less assistance in making things happen. When I directed a play there, I had to take my turn manning the box office and concession stand, which I really hated. I was the board treasurer for several years and lined up a grant to put in a more adequate lighting system. But the principals at Brush Creek were impossibly provincial and set in their ways, and there were hardly any actors I wanted to work with. Actors with any alternative preferred a theatre with running water.

Nonetheless, I wrote them a play called *Deep in the Woods*, imagining the little stage transformed into the interior of my cabin in the northern Berkshires, where a group of urban friends come together after an electrical disaster has destroyed New York City. Given a date in early 2007, I put myself into gear and started pulling it together. Casting was a huge challenge, and I got no help from the members of the theatre. In the end I was unable to cast two of the key roles, even badly, and I was forced to cancel the production the day before rehearsals were to begin, which was a wrenching disappointment. In truth I think the play needed work, and it's probably just as well it didn't go on.

Doing plays in New York and Santa Barbara was fun, but I wanted to stay home with Carol—have my cake and eat it too: Bob Dylan said you can. So a couple of years after *Deep in the Woods* fizzled out, I wrote another play for Brush Creek, thinking ahead this time about how to do it with the actors I could get. *Summer Lightning* draws on my memories of the Caffè Cino, where I did my first theatre work in New York—a loving tribute, comical in character. The title was arbitrarily lifted from a P. G. Wodehouse novel.

I drove over to the theatre and let myself in several times while I was writing *Summer Lightning*, walking through the scenes as they developed, figuring out how to fit them onto the tiny stage. The set would be elaborate. To the audience's right was a corner of the Caffè Cino, with Joe Cino behind the

counter at the big espresso machine, a tiny cafe table and chairs, a viewport into the light booth. To the left was the crowded dressing room, seen through a mirror bordered with light bulbs. In the center were two slender Greek columns and a fake rock on a thrust stage, the minimal set for the play-within-the-play, which was my adaptation of Racine's *Phèdre*—a tribute to Harry Koutoukas's *Medea*, done at the Cino in 1964. The action bounced back and forth between the cafe and the dressing room, with *Phèdre* in the middle.

It was an odd show but the product of genuine feeling—the Caffè Cino had been important in my life, shaping my idea of the spirit in which I always wanted to do theatre, playful and serious at once. Of all the Greek tragedies, I cherish a particular fondness for *Phèdre* and enjoyed translating Racine. *Summer Lightning* came out well—I was delighted with it. I had a good, game group and did what I wanted to do.

Hamlet in Love

My "happy Hamlet" was born from a conversation over lunch with actor-director Norman Gouveia, a Brush Creek stalwart. They were looking for royalty-free plays to do, and I suggested Shakespeare. *Hamlet* is always good, but when I thought about it, a full production was impractical for several reasons. I gave some thought to devising a small-cast version, the way I had cut *A Midsummer Night's Dream* to a manageable size. Then I saw an excellent five-actor *Hamlet* in Portland—no need to do that again.

In the event, I wrote my own alternate version of *Hamlet*. I love the character of Hamlet, but I hate what happens to him in the story Shakespeare tells. Maybe Shakespeare got it wrong. I never trusted the Ghost. I invented an entirely different story about Hamlet and Ophelia and his mother and her two husbands with a happy ending. No one died.

I had my Hamlet, a talented, charismatic young man named Kory Crosen, who had played Lysander in my *Midsummer Night's Dream* when he was still in high school and Theramenes to Alfred's Hippolytus in *Summer Lightning*. Kory was the right age and very model of the beautiful Hamlet in my

mind's eye. He was not literary and completely at sea in the initial reading. Alfred, cast as Laertes, was appalled. I held solo rehearsals with Kory every week for two months before I began rehearsing the rest of the cast, and by then he had a good grasp of the character and language. Alfred came for the rehearsal period and three weekends of performances and used the play as a stepping stone in moving from Santa Barbara to Portland. Norman was Polonius. I wrote Gertrude for Betty Ann Prior, a high-spirited comedienne who had been in two of my other shows. When Betty Ann dropped out, I persuaded my friend Kelley Morehouse, who was already on board as the stage manager, to take on the part. She had never acted before—literally never. Kelley was alarmingly inept in early rehearsals, but she hung in with me and gave a fine and funny performance as Gertrude.

Hamlet in Love would have looked hopelessly amateurish on the Brush Creek stage. Instead my new producing entity, Re-Genesis, presented it in the black box theatre at the new Silverton

High School, a usefully set-up room behind the main stage designed for acting classes and close-up performances. Doing *Hamlet in Love* was a happy if taxing process, which in the end came  out more or less as I envisioned it. I gave my play the simplest of bare-stage productions, a throne upstage on one side, a swag of red brocade, a bench on the other for the garden scene. Karyl Carlson, our invaluable costume designer, stepped up as stage manager and was perfectly wonderful. Apart from that I had to do everything including the light setup myself. With a painful, failing hip, I was up and down the ladder to the grid innumerable times, feeling very sorry for myself. It was worth it, for sure, but the psychic and physical effort of willing the whole thing into existence, getting it right, bending everybody to my will, was too much. I have not had another idea of a play I want to put on. *Hamlet in Love* may be my last play.

I started writing this text in mid-July. Winter came, chilly, raining, dark; now it is summer again, sunny and warm. I keep myself busy writing, playing music, publishing books, loving and living. I am not in the theatre anymore, I suppose, but the theatre is still in me.

Photo Credits

Cover — At Theater for the New City, New York, during rehearsals for *Trouble,* December 2005 (photo by Alfred Smith)

Page 14 — Diane Fisher, Louis Zetter, Deborah Lee, Lou Waldon, and Marva Abraham in *Three Sisters Who Are Not Sisters* by Gertrude Stein, at a benefit for the Caffè Cino, presented by Ron Link at the Sullivan Street Playhouse, 1965

Page 15 — Cynthia Harris, Jim Barbosa, Lee Worley, John Kramer, and John Coe in *Icarus's Mother* by Sam Shepard, Caffè Cino, 1965 (photo by Conrad Ward)

Page 17 — Ed Setrakian and Barbara Vann in *The Next Thing*, presented by the Open Theatre at La Mama, 1966

Page 18 — Joyce Aaron in *More! More! I Want More!* at a benefit for and at La Mama, presented by Robert Patrick, 1965 (photo by James D. Gossage)

Page 25 — Charles Stanley as Tiny Tim, Arnold Horton as Bob Cratchitt, and Ondine (Robert Olivo) as Scrooge in *Chas. Dickens's Christmas Carol* by Søren Agenoux, Caffè Cino, 1966 (photo by Billy Name)

Page 26 — Arnold Horton, Søren Agenoux, and Charles Stanley in *Chas. Dickens's Christmas Carol*

Page 27 — Olimpio Vasconcelos and Ondine on my peculiarly shaped stage in *Donovan's Johnson* by Søren Agenoux, Caffè Cino, 1968

Page 29 — Alfred Brooks and Maxine Munt, from a promotional flyer for the Munt-Brooks Dance Company, c. 1954

Page 31 — John P. Dodd in the title role of *The Life of Juanita Castro* by Ronald Tavel, with Gay Boswell, Carol Marie Book, and Anita Newman as Fidel, Raul, and Che Guevara, The Changing Scene, Denver, 1968

Page 33 — Lucy Silvay and Rob Thirkield in *Hurrricane of the Eye* by Emanuel Peluso, set by Jerry Joyner, La Mama, 1969

Page 38 — Diane McAfee and Edward Barton in *A Dog's Love,* opera with music by John Herbert McDowell, set by Charles Terrel, La Mama, 1971

Page 39 — Playing the harpsichord for *A Dog's Love*

Page 40 — Lucy Silvay in *Tony*, La Mama, 1971

Page 41 — Patricia Madsen and Melanie Kern in *Peas*, The Changing Scene, Denver, 1971

Page 43 — Dennis Stull, Sarah Marsh, Burt Kruse, Greg Boyle, and John Simcox in *XXXXX* by William M. Hoffman, The Changing Scene, 1971

Page 45 — Nevele Adams and Charles Stanley in an atypical moment from *Country Music*, Theatre Genesis, 1972 (photo by Conrad Ward)

Page 47 — *Bigfoot* by Ronald Tavel, Theatre Genesis, 1972: Nancy McCormick, Scott Gordon, and Walter Hadler; Amlin Gray and Nancy McCormick; Ben Kushner, Paul Pierog, Scott Gordon, and Billy Natbony; Billy Natbony, Harvey Tavel, and Ben Kushner

Page 49 — Ben Masters and Bill Moor in *Tango Palace* by María Irene Fornés, Theatre Genesis, 1973

Page 50 — Patricia Madsen, John Simcox, and Nancy Mangus at the table, Erica Bramesco (musician), Dennis Stull, and Melanie Kern upstage in *Double Solitaire*, The Changing Scene, Denver, 1973

Page 53 — front: Michele Hawley, Ondine, Jimmy Camicia; back: John Smead, Charles Stanley, the author, and Georgia Lee on the *Prussian Suite* set at Theatre Genesis, 1974

Page 54 — Jimmy Camicia in *Prussian Suite*

Page 56 — Directing Michele Hawley, Nancy Mangus, Dennis Stull, Jane Larew, and Bill Dohme (plus musicians up in the trees) on the unfinished set by Charles Vanderpool for *A Wedding Party*,

The Changing Scene, Denver, 1974

Page 62 — Bill Bolender in *Krapp's Last Tape* by Samuel Beckett, Plaza Theatre, Taos, New Mexico, 1978

Page 63 — Rehearsing *West Side Story* at the Taos Community Auditorium, 1978

Page 67 — Dennis Pinette in *Heavy Pockets*, Living Room Theatre, Westerly, Rhode Island, 1983

Page 70 — Dick Spahn and Gwynne Van Seenus in *Come In Here* (excerpted from *Half Life*), Ensemble Theatre Company, Santa Barbara, 1994

Page 76 — Jaime Arze and Pamela Eliasoph in *Curse of the Starving Class* by Sam Shepard, Connecticut College, 1985

Page 81 — left, clockwise from upper left: Ilion Troya, Joanie Fritz Zosike, Gary Brackett, Alan Arenius, and Laura Kolb in *I and I* by Else Lasker-Schüler, The Living Theatre, Berlin, 1990; right: Jerry Goralnick as Hitler (photos by Ira Cohen)

Page 86 — Judith Malina and Hanon Reznikov in *The Zero Method* by Hanon Reznikov, The Living Theatre (Third Street), 1992

Page 89 — David M. Brainard and Kinsey Packard in *Fast Forward*, Center Stage Theater, Santa Barbara, 1999

Page 92 — Rojan Disparte in *Buried Child* by Sam Shepard, Lobero Theatre, Santa Barbara, 1999 (photographs for Genesis West by David Bazemore)

Page 93 — Robert Riechel Jr., Rojan Disparte, Kinsey Packard, Michael Rathbone, Larry Williams, and Howie Lotker in *Buried Child*

Page 94 — Kinsey Packard and ClaireMarie Mallory in *Featuring Loretta* by George F. Walker, Center Stage Theater, Santa Barbara, 2000

Page 95 — ClaireMarie Mallory, Leslie Gangl Howe, Kinsey Packard, and Erica Kylander-Clark in *Escape from Happiness* by

George F. Walker, Lobero Theatre, Santa Barbara, 2000

Page 96 — Leslie Gangl Howe and David M. Brainard in *Escape from Happiness*

Page 97 — Laurel Lyle in *Dogs Bark All Night*, Center Stage Theater, Santa Barbara, 2000

Page 98 — David M. Brainard, Laurel Lyle, Steven Gonzales, and ClaireMarie Mallory in *Dogs Bark All Night*

Page 99 — George Backman, Erica Kylander-Clark, Drew Murphy, and Ken Gilbert in *The Danube* by María Irene Fornés, Center Stage Theater, Santa Barbara, 2001

Page 100 — Drew Murphy, Erica Kylander-Clark, and George Backman in *The Danube*

Page 101 — Robert Lesser in *Krapp's Last Tape* by Samuel Beckett, Center Stage Theater, Santa Barbara, 2002

Page 104 — Geren Piltz, Fred Lehto, and Paula Re in *Turnip Family Secrets*, music by Josef Woodard, Center Stage Theater, Santa Barbara, 2002; Geoffrey Bell as the Giant

Page 105 — Geren Piltz and Geoffrey Bell as the Fairy, "flying"

Page 106 — Geoffrey Bell, Paula Re, Fred Lehto, and Geren Piltz in Venice at the end of *Turnip Family Secrets*

Page 110 — *A Midsummer Night's Dream (Abbreviated)*, Abiqua Country Estate, Silverton, Oregon, 2004: Steve Slemenda and Betty Ann Prior as Oberon and Titania; Betty Ann Prior with Phil Baker as Bottom; Hallie Day as Puck, with Fairy

Page 112 — Cast of *The Flight of the Butter Boy* by Guy J. Jackson, Brush Creek Players, Silverton, Oregon, 2005: standing from left, Lydia Quinones, Richard Arias Jr., Nancy White, Abrian Velarde, Mares Bradberry, Jacob Dickson; sitting, Laura Jean Riches, Michele Dahlum, Alfred St. John Smith, Cierston St. Paul, Gary Roelofs; front, Taylor Bradberry

Page 114 — Kathryn Chilson as Tess Byerson in *Trouble*, Theater for the New City, New York, 2006; Renato R. Biribin as Big Boy and Alfred St. John Smith as Dickie

Page 115 — Kathryn Chilson, Alfred St. John Smith, and Jimmy Camicia as Sandy Morphol in *Trouble;* Dino Roscigno as Randy and Joshua Levine as the Gaoler

Page 117 — Meredith McMinn, Leslie Gangl Howe, and Tom Hinshaw in *Blue Heart* by Caryl Churchill, produced and directed by Maurice Lord, Center Stage Theater, Santa Barbara, 2005

Page 118 — Tiffany Rose Brown and Chris Turner in *Far Away* by Caryl Churchill, Center Stage Theater, Santa Barbara, 2006

Page 119 — Laurel Lyle as Janice in *Bad Dog,* Center Stage Theater, Santa Barbara, 2007

Page 120 — *Bad Dog and Other Plays,* Center Stage Theater, Santa Barbara, 2007: Susan Keller in *More! More! I Want More!;* Alfred St. John Smith and Laurel Lyle in *Fast Forward*

Page 121 — Laurel Lyle, David M. Brainard, Suzanne Bodine, Alfred St. John Smith, Susan Keller, and Tom Petra in *Point Blank*

Page 123 — *Summer Lightning,* Brush Creek Playhouse, Silverton, Oregon, 2009: Kory Crosen, Vere McCarty, Norman Gouveia, Tavis Evans, and Alison White in the dressing room; Norman Gouveia and Jacob Dickson in the cafe; Betty Ann Prior, Kory Crosen, and Vere McCarty in *Phèdre* (photos by William Naiditch)

Page 125 — *Hamlet in Love,* Black Box Theater, Silverton High School, Silverton, Oregon, 2010: Kory Crosen as Hamlet with Dianne Bates as Ophelia; Vere McCarty, Kory Crosen, and Kelley Morehouse; Alfred St. John Smith and Dianne Bates; Norman Gouveia as Polonius

Page 126 — Directing *Hamlet in Love*

www.ingramcontent.com/pod-product-compliance
Lightning Source LLC
LaVergne TN
LVHW041256080426
835510LV00009B/761